PRAYERS

OF THE

PEOPLE

Ordering Information:

Quantity sales. Special discounts are available on quantity purchases by corporations, associations, and others. For details, contact the publisher at the address above.

Printed in the United States of America. First Edition.

ISBN 978-0-9974289-0-2

This title is also available as an ebook.

1. REL012080 RELIGION / Christian Life / Prayer
2. REL012120 RELIGION / Christian Life / Spiritual Growth
3. REL012020 RELIGION / Christian Life / Devotional

For more information, visit: www.redeemer.com

TABLE *of*
CONTENTS

GIVE ME
A STOUT HEART
to bear my own burdens.

GIVE ME
A WILLING HEART
to bear the burdens of others.

GIVE ME
A BELIEVING HEART
to cast all burdens upon Thee, O Lord.

— JOHN BAILLIE

TO THE
PRAYING CONGREGANTS
of
REDEEMER
PRESBYTERIAN CHURCH

ACKNOWLEDGMENTS

PUTTING TOGETHER A BOOK is hard work, especially a book that is written by more than five dozen people. Sometimes the things most worth doing take the most work. I want to acknowledge and thank the team of people who made this book a reality.

The first and biggest acknowledgment goes to everyone who contributed a prayer to this project. I want to express my sincere gratitude to them for trusting me with stewarding the publication of these most personal and sacred words. In the index, you can find the list of 62 people whose prayers were included in this volume. However, we had just as many people submit prayers of equal substance and depth. I wish we could have included them all.

These individuals represent an even greater cloud of witnesses to the hope of the gospel throughout New York City and throughout every city, who daily lift their voices in prayer for their families, friends, neighbors, and co-workers. Having had the privilege of reading through the prayers of hundreds of New Yorkers over the past months, I have come to believe that there is an invisible but true and humble faith that resides just below the surface of countless people I pass daily on the streets. If anything, I am now more convinced that the image of God is reflected in the face of every person, and that more people have more spiritual depth than I might naturally imagine.

The team at Frontier Press was a tremendous partner in visualizing what this book could be and how to bring it to completion. I can't imagine a more professional, gracious, or supportive publishing partner than Jason Ashlock and his team of Allison Blake, who managed our project, Chris Porter, who designed the cover, and Katherine Schutt, who went above and beyond copy-editing to improve my work.

Early on, Bruce Terrell saw the value in this project and supported it throughout. Kathy Keller read every word and helped keep the gospel at the center. Kelsey Heinz helped with the initial management of the project, bringing order to the website and the submission process.

Later on, Carolann Chaplin and Cregan Cooke helped conceptualize the cover and final version of the book. Their support and partnership couldn't have come at a more welcome time.

As I mention in the introduction, Amanda Lindemann and the Redeemer West Side Kids Community Group prayer team inspired this project. I am thankful to them for their example, and I am thankful for everyone who has helped and prayed for this book to become a reality.

— *Maxwell Anderson*

FOREWORD

BY TIMOTHY J. KELLER

THERE'S NOTHING MORE IMPORTANT THAN PRAYER.
You can't know God without prayer. You can know a lot about him, of course, but you can't know God personally without a prayer life.

You can't truly know yourself without prayer. It is only in the light of God's presence that you can finally see your heart as it is.

You can't really love other people as well without prayer. If you have started praying regularly for someone, and then you meet with him or her, you will see how much more engaged your heart is. Love may lead you to pray, but then prayer profoundly deepens and enhances love.

Finally, you can't really get through the troubles, disappointments, and tragedies of life without prayer. This is the message of one of the most famous passages in the Bible: Psalm 23. We will only walk through the dark valleys without fear if we know his presence in prayer. Suffering usually makes you more anxious, more hardened and cynical, but through prayer it can make you wiser, deeper, kinder, and even more joyful.

It is also extraordinarily important to listen to other people pray.

Several writers have noticed that if you are part of a circle of friends, and one of the friends moves away, you lose more than just that particular person. If you lose friend A, you also lose, as it were, the part of friend B that only friend A could bring out. You can know an individual human being better in a community than simply one-on-one. Why? Because one-on-one you only see the part of the person that you draw out, and not all the other aspects of him or her that are visible in other settings with other people.

Now if it is the case that the fullness of a finite individual human can't be known and drawn out by only one person, how much more true is that of God? Every one of us, because of our unique experiences and traits, perceives certain facets of God's infinite beauty and glory. But no one of us can glimpse even a fraction of the whole. Only if you worship with others and hear others pray will you begin to get a fuller view of God's magnificence. Solitary faith, something that the Bible knows nothing about, will always produce a distorted view of God.

That is why *Prayers of the People* is such a helpful and important volume. In it, you hear a remarkable diversity of people, from many walks of life, in a variety of human circumstances, all praising, confessing, thanking, and petitioning God. Listen carefully, and you will find that each soul is communicating her unique vision of God to you. And so we are enriched as we can be in no other way. Read this volume, turn some of your friends' prayers into your own, and so you will grow in grace and in the knowledge of the Father and of his son (John 17:3; 2 Peter 3:18.)

Also read this volume so that you can be part of the vision of the Rise campaign: that New York would be a more just, beautiful, merciful, and kind city because the people within it are living more and more for God and their neighbor. This is a vision that must begin and end in prayer. It begins in prayer because we could never accomplish all we hope to do in our own power. It ends in prayer because only that way will we increasingly become like our God who calls for the peace and flourishing of the city.

THE CALL TO PRAYER

Then you will call on me and come and pray to me,
and I will listen to you. You will seek me
and find me when you seek me with all your heart.

JEREMIAH 29: 12–13

G OD WOULD LIKE to have a word with us. That much, at least, is clear. I do not mean he would like to have a word in the sense that he aims to give us a stern lecture. I mean that when you read the scriptures of the Old and New Testament, you cannot help but come away with the impression that the immortal God seems to want to be in conversation with the all-too-mortal *us*. He wants us to listen to him, but oddly—and it is odd if you think about it—he also wants to listen to us.

This is odd in the same way it would be odd for a woman or man to be interested in hearing the thoughts of a mosquito. After all, if there is an immortal, omnipotent Creator of the Universe, then we humans must be, by analogy, even less to him than a bug is to us. And yet the scriptures paint a different picture altogether of the way God would like us to relate to him.

We are encouraged, by none other than Jesus himself, to call God "our Father" or, more uncomfortably, "Papa." (Romans 8:15). The Bible says we are to be "children of God" (Romans 8:16) and "sons of God" (Galatians 3:26). It depicts God as gladly hearing our earnest, if often uninformed and selfish, prayers:

Or which one of you, if his son asks him for bread, will give him a stone?
Or if he asks for a fish, will give him a serpent? If you, then, who are evil,
know how to give good gifts to your children, how much more will
your Father who is in heaven give good things to those who ask him!

MATTHEW 7:9–11

Of course, if you are a Christian, you've known this for years. You know it so well, in fact, that you've actually forgotten it. Or more precisely, you have forgotten how arresting an idea this is. Familiarity breeds unfamiliarity. As a result, your prayers have gone flat. Stale. Talking with God is not electric as it once was. It has become a bore. Visiting the ocean is a great adventure for a woman from the Midwest who never sees it. She might sit for hours staring at it, just appreciating the beauty. For the one who lives near the coast, however, the sea may fade into the background landscape. She *knows* it is beautiful and refreshing, but she rarely makes time to go, because, you know, you can always do that some other time. For now there are more urgent things to do. There are emails to write! Meetings to sit through! Dishes to do! You can always pray some other time.

We could go on at length about the importance of talking and listening to God in prayer as shown throughout the pages of the Bible: how God's greatest commandment is to love him (Matthew 22:35-40); how we are commanded to pray without ceasing (Philippians 4:6-7); how Jesus himself prioritized prayer (Mark 1:35); how God hears our prayers and answers them even when we don't know the right words to say (Romans 8:26-27). Reading these verses is a bit like having someone grasp you by the shoulders and gently shake you awake when you've started to doze. You may come alive with a start.

However, this book is not so much about *why* we pray but *how*. It is a tool and an aid for those who would like to grow more consistent and confident in what may seem the most uncomfortable of conversations. This book is not a set of propositions that you read once and then set down; it is a collection of examples for you to read, ruminate on, build off of, and explore over and over again. It is "show" more than "tell."

Why We Need Models of Prayer

Prayer is learned by example and by doing rather than by teaching. Consider the book of Psalms, which has been called the prayer book of the Bible. The Psalms do not teach us how to pray by telling, but by showing us the way. They are a collection of 150 examples of prayer. They are remarkable in their honesty and in the sweep of emotion they cover. In them, we find expressions of praise and delight, but also of sadness and fear, humility and courage. As the musician Bono said, "What's so powerful about the Psalms are, as well as they're being gospel and songs of praise, they are also the blues."

The Psalms demonstrate ways of praying for so many of the situations you may find yourself in. If you are anxious and feeling insecure, reading Psalm 139 models a way to preach to your heart the encouraging truth that God is never far away. If you are feeling guilty and ashamed, Psalm 51 models how to confess your own shallowness and beg God's mercy. If you are desperate and lost, Psalm 69 gives evidence that you are not alone and shares a model for praying for help in the midst of your confusion.

Jesus taught his followers to pray in the same way. When his disciples begged him to teach them how to pray, Jesus did not give them a list of principles or rules or aphorisms. He did not hand them a cookbook or manual of instructions. He simply prayed and let them listen in. He said, to paraphrase, "If you want to pray, it ought to sound something like this" and then he began, "Our Father..." And for centuries the church has prayed these exact words as the most common way of addressing God.

Beyond the Lord's Prayer and the Psalms, the church has used liturgical prayers for centuries as a method of instruction in prayer. One of the most famous examples is the *Book of Common Prayer.* As beautiful as any hymn, collects like those of Thomas Cranmer offer rich expressions of praise, contrition, and gratitude to God. Going through these liturgical prayers week by week has taught generations of Christians how to talk with God.

In some Protestant circles, liturgical prayers arouse suspicion of over emphasizing ritual at the expense of authentic faith. This spirit carries over today into a belief, among some, that prayer must be informal and spontaneous to be authentically from the heart.

I have some sympathy for those concerns, but I would say that this is an area where the right path may not be to decide "either/or." The wise choice may be "both/and." Allow me to share an analogy. In my relationship with my wife, I ought to share with her my hopes and desires. I ought to admit to her when I am wrong. I ought to tell her I appreciate her for who she is and what she does for our family.

Through the years of our marriage, I have done these things both informally in everyday conversation and formally in the form of cards, letters, and poems. I can tell you that if I only wrote her my feelings, our relationship would likely feel a bit overly formal. On the other hand, if I never took the time to put on paper a richer, more thoughtful expression of my love, I would never do justice to the depths of feeling I have for her. I would always be fumbling for the words. I'm convinced our relationship is healthiest when I do some combination of both.

Perhaps our relationships with God aren't so dissimilar. Many times the best way to talk with him is extemporaneous—you know what is on your heart to say and you say it conversationally. Other times, however, your mind is in a fog. You know you should bring yourself to God, but you don't know what to say. You might be aided in prayer by allowing someone to take you by the hand and lead the way.

The theologian N.T. Wright affirms the helpfulness of words composed by someone else this way:

> Indeed, the idea that I must always find my own words, that I must generate my own devotion from scratch every morning, that unless I think of new words I must be spiritually lazy or deficient—that has the all-too-familiar sign of human pride, of "doing it my way": of, yes, works-righteousness. Good liturgy—other people's prayers, whether for corporate or individual use—can be, should be, a sign and means of grace, an occasion of humility (accepting that someone else has said, better than I can, what I deeply want to express) and gratitude.[i]

Before reading that, I had never thought other people's prayers as a "means of grace" and "an occasion of humility." But there are many who feel nervous about praying aloud, especially in a group, fearful that they will sound foolish. For them, the guidance of a written prayer is a grace. On the other hand, there are many who feel comfortable praying out loud and extemporaneously. I am one of them, but if I am honest, it is hard for me not to have my prayers tainted by a concern for what listeners will think of my words. *Do I sound wise? Humble? Theologically correct?* A written prayer is an occasion for humility.

Every Sunday at our church, the congregation reads aloud a common written prayer of confession, then we are given time to pray silently. I

[i] Wright, N.T. *Simply Christian*. HarperOne. 2010.

always re-read the confession prayer and pray it as my own personal confession, changing every "we" into an "I" as I go. Every week, I am thankful for the guide, because I wouldn't be nearly as honest with God or myself without the prompting of someone who had thought about it enough beforehand to write it down.

When I was in college, my mother gave me a copy of John Baillie's classic *A Diary of Private Prayer*. It was a revelation. In this collection of a Scottish pastor's prayers from the middle of the 20th century, I found language that was beautifully written, theologically deep, yet relevant to many of the concerns I saw in the world and felt in my life. The prayers balanced elements of praise, thankfulness, confession, and supplication. They frequently quoted and meditated on passages from scripture. They covered a breadth of topics that I was too impatient and uncreative to pray for on my own. He prayed for everyone, from "the overworked and the unemployed," to "those who labor with their minds," to "those who labor with their hands." He prayed for all who serve in pulpits, and all who serve in the home. Before reading this book, I had been mainly just praying for *me*.

For months, I read those prayers daily, and as I did, I found my own private prayers changing as a result of following his example. I began praying more in response to scripture. I began consciously praying for more people and situations outside of my own life and experience. I spent less time asking for things I wanted and more time admitting my need for grace. My prayers grew deeper, and the matters they concerned grew broader. I began to feel a greater joy in prayer. I had lifted my gaze from my own shoelaces to see the broad expanse of the world before me, and it was exciting and satisfying. I did not think of it at the time, but this experience was the seed that germinated into the book you are holding.

How This Book Came to Be

This book came about somewhat by accident. Some parents in our church had begun a weekday Kids Community Group to get the elementary children together for a midweek time of singing, games, and Bible study. The program became well-attended, attracting both children from the church and their classmates at school.

One of the mothers, Amanda, recruited a team of parents to pray for the children and their teachers each week. She asked me to join. I said yes, and soon received an email from her sent to the seven or eight of us she had recruited. She included a list of all the children and teachers so that we could pray for them by name, and she wrote an original prayer for the children that we could read and use as the basis of our own prayers.

When the email came in, I was at my desk and put aside my work to spend a few minutes reading and praying through it. I was expecting to go through the exercise rather quickly, do my duty, check the box, and move on with my day. I wasn't expecting to be moved by beauty. But I was.

The prayer was straightforward but beautiful in its sincerity and honesty. It was packed with scripture. It was specific. And it was filled with praise. Reading it, I was humbled by the obvious fullness of her prayer life. Then it hit me that I shouldn't be surprised. Someone leading an active prayer group in New York is likely to have a robust spiritual life.

In some parts of the country, Christianity is part and parcel of the local culture. Christian faith may not be universal in those areas, but it is broadly assumed that praying and Bible reading are part of life, much in the way that it is assumed one has some affinity for sweet tea or certain types of barbecue. You might call these environments "culturally Christian," where one might go to church for social or business reasons as much as (or in lieu of) spiritual reasons. The majority of people say they are Christian, but it's not always clear who actually believes what. These are places where many people assume being Christian is pretty much the same as being an American.

New York City is not one of these places.

Self-identifying as a Christian in New York City means that one belongs to a smaller minority group. Very few people attend a church service on a Sunday morning. Some beautiful old churches stand relatively empty. Christians aren't persecuted in New York, but they score no social points for attending church on Sunday. One does not choose to become a Christian in New York because it is comfortable or because it might get you somewhere professionally.

Thus, when you meet a churchgoing New Yorker, you have likely met someone who is serious about her faith. She has probably been challenged many times by her friends and colleagues about her beliefs, forcing her to think hard, study, and come to her own conclusions about her beliefs. In other words, spiritual maturity has been hard-earned. It often exhibits the fruit of an unusual amount of prayer and theological reflection. New York City is something of a refiner's fire in this regard.

This is not to say that those of us living in the city are saints—far from it. The city feeds on personal ambition. Our anthem is still: *If I can make it there, I'll make it anywhere.* The city whispers promises in our ears that the hunger we feel inside can be satisfied by money or sex or power or fame. I suppose these are temptations common in every city. In New York, they are simply amplified. And none of us are fully immune to the seductive power of their charms.

Because of this, rather than in spite of it, those who "make it" in New York, spiritually speaking, are well-acquainted with the vocabulary of grace. Having experienced both the empty idolatry of success and the broken feeling of failure, we have grown to see the city for what it is: a place of tremendous beauty and opportunity, a place broken by self-centeredness and greed, a place where redemption is possible.

So perhaps I should not have been surprised by the beauty of this mother's prayer. But I was, and that prayer became both an occasion for humility and a means of grace. As I sat at my desk reading this mother's prayer for our children, I began thinking that our church probably has dozens and dozens of people like her, who daily walk the upward road, who know how to pray. I decided that those are the people I want to learn from and emulate. That's where this project was born.

Three months later, I stood in front of our church and asked if people would share their prayers to create a new book of prayer that could be used by anyone seeking to deeper their spiritual life. The idea was to create a modern prayer book that addressed today's world and concerns across a wide spectrum of perspectives. Dozens and dozens of people responded from throughout New York. They are attorneys and accountants, doctors, dancers, and investors. They are mothers, fathers, single people, and people who have lived long enough to have lost spouses and loved ones. They are people of different races and different parts of the city, the country, and the world. Together they form a mosaic of God at work in the lives of people in neighborhoods and vocations throughout the city. The whole book amounts to a wonderful and beautiful testimony to the poignancy of the gospel in every sphere of life and to the reach of God's work into every square inch of creation.

We had far more print-worthy submissions than we were able to include in this volume. This is the best kind of problem for an editor to have. There are many I would have loved to include but that did not fit well within the constraints of the project. I am grateful for everyone who participated by sharing their prayers, whether they are included here or not. It was a pleasure to read them all.

How To Read This Book

You may read this book any way you like. However, I suggest you use it as a month-long plan for spiritual growth. I believe that many people would like to have a richer spiritual life but are so distracted with work, family, email, and other commitments that they edge out room for stillness, contemplation, and prayer. To get past this, it helps to have a plan. Here is the one I would recommend.

Make a commitment to invest in your spiritual life during this next month. If you would like to feel less hurried and frazzled, if you want to be more focused on the important things, resolve to do something about it. This book is designed to be used twice a day as a guide for your personal times of prayer and reflection. It is organized into 31 days, with a morning prayer and an evening prayer for each day. If you were to use it twice a day for a month, I believe you would see your prayer life grow deeper and your entire life would feel more spiritually rich.

To give yourself the best chance on following through with your resolution, take a moment to think through your morning and visualize what you will have to do to spend 10 minutes in the morning going through the morning prayer. Would you need to get up 10 minutes earlier? Is there a window you can count on your kids not interrupting you? Can you do it first thing when you get to the office? It will have to fit in somewhere. The question is where? Think that through.

Go through the same exercise for the evening prayer. Will you read it at dinner? As you lie in bed before turning out the lights? Pick a time and try to stick with it for the month.

Each prayer begins with a word of introduction about the prayer and the author. It is followed by a brief selection from scripture, then the prayer itself. My recommendation is to read the introduction straight through. When you get to the scripture, read it slowly, then before moving on, pause and think about it. What did you just read? What does it mean? If it is true, how does it affect you? Then go back and read through the scripture again. The selections are short, so it won't take too much time. The risk is in approaching this as an activity to efficiently check off the list without taking the time to let it affect you.

When you come to the prayer, do not read it simply as an interesting thing that someone else wrote. Read it as if it were your own prayer. In the editing process, we tried to phrase the prayers so that a reader could read them as his or her own words. I hope you will read them that way and experience them, to paraphrase N.T. Wright, as an occasion for humility and as a true means of grace in your life.

PRAYERS *of the* PEOPLE

FIRST DAY
MORNING

In this prayer, the writer remembers his place in the created world and the preeminent place of our Creator. Before he begins his work, the writer pauses to remember the work God has done—in him and all around him. He requests that he might *remember the greatness* of God's works so that he might *delight* in the study of creation. Delight isn't an act of will. It doesn't come out of nowhere. It comes from realizing the good work God has done first, and responding. As you pray through it, consider what is the "lab" of work that you are entering today? What experiments will you run and in what ways might you study God's work and character anew?

〜

The morning prayer is written by Braxton, who was born and raised in Pittsfield, Illinois. Now a postdoctoral researcher in mechanical engineering, he studies the intersection of music and physics through acoustics and audio systems.

"My first prayer was when I was very young, sitting under a very old tree in the yard at my grandmother's farm. I had a strong sense that God loved me and wanted to be my friend, and I prayed that he would take care of me and my family."

Great are the works of the LORD, studied by all who delight in them.
Full of splendor and majesty is his work, and his righteousness endures
forever. He has caused his wondrous works to be remembered;
the Lord is gracious and merciful.

PSALM 111:2–4

As I enter the lab today,
    please let me remember
the greatness of your works
    that I may delight in the study of
    your creation.

I stand on the shoulders
    of giants who have come before:
let me not rest in their actions
    but continue striving to discover
one more sliver of your creation.

As your Spirit sustains the world
    from moment to moment,
please sustain my spirit
    through one more day
        without results;
renew the sense of wonder you
        first gave me
    when I gazed with new eyes on
    your creation.

Let me not worship gold in the hills
    or stars in the sky
or the praise of people in the world,
    as though they possessed
        the answers
to the mysteries I face,
    as though they were not also
a part of your creation.

Give me a thankful heart that
    though I am tiny and my tools
        are clumsy,
by your gracious arrangement
    of the order of all things,
I am allowed to tread the spiral path
    of ever-increasing knowledge
        and truth
to witness the glory of your creation.

Remind me daily of the strangeness
    that through the gift of reason
I am allowed to understand a portion
    of a raindrop on a tree branch,
or the power that moves the cosmos,
    yet I am as much a part of
that same creation as they are.

And when I fall short of
        those standards
    of absolute beauty, simplicity,
        and consistency
that are everywhere displayed in
        your work,
let me never forget
    that because of your love for me,
you also became a part of
        your creation.

Amen.

FIRST DAY
EVENING

At day's end, feeling weary of the distracting clamor of the world, this prayer's writer confesses the restlessness of her heart, remembers the peace offered by the Lord, and rests in the promise of Sabbath. The sad truth is that we can acknowledge the greatness of God, who gives every good thing, whose blessings abound, and yet still feel restless. We need new eyes to see his blessings instead of focusing only on our problems.

The evening prayer is written by Katharine, a freelance editor and mother of two who was born and raised in Richmond, Virginia. Katharine moved to New York in 1993; four years later, she visited Redeemer for the first time with the man who would become her husband.

"I don't remember a time when God was not a part of my life, but I can't say I took an active role in my faith until I felt drawn back to church after I moved to New York. I genuinely prayed the Lord's Prayer as a child, with my parents and alone at bedtime. However, I didn't truly learn how to pray until being in community at Redeemer where I was encouraged to pray out loud. It was uncomfortable at first, but transformed my prayer life over time."

My presence will go with you,
and I will give you rest.

EXODUS 33:14

DEAR LORD, HEAVENLY FATHER, Almighty God, you are my strength and my salvation. Your mercy is boundless and your grace is immeasurable. You give me every good thing; your blessings abound. Your peace passes all understanding, and yet...I am restless.

The world calls and I follow; my heart is too easily led away from you. I feel burdened by my sin and detached, yet I don't lay my troubles at your feet as you've asked me to. I want to go my own way, but time and again, that way has proven destructive. In particular, I confess today _____.

Dear Lord, my soul is weary. Teach me how to find rest in you and you only. Deliver me from the whiplash of indecision and anxiety and show me how your love and light and truth are the only way. This city is home to writers and editors. I pray the stories they tell would be true. I recognize the draft I have written for my own life needs your editing hand. Remind me of your loving-kindness and of the sacrifice of your Son. Show me where I am putting my hope in false idols instead of in him. Recraft my narrative about what is important, such that you regain the central place.

Humble me, dear Lord, so that I understand my Sabbath needs and nurture the seed of hope you've planted in me so it will bear fruit. Deepen my heart's desire for you so that I seek time in prayer and meditation and push aside the distracted busyness of this world. Focus my mind and heart so much on you that when I move out into the world, I see your blessings instead of my problems and follow your path instead of my own. Spur me on, dear Lord, with the knowledge that your Word is living and active and that I may always find you there, in every circumstance, if I look.

I ask this all in your Son's precious name, Amen.

SECOND DAY
MORNING

In this morning prayer, the writer recites many of the attributes and excellencies of God. It is easy for us to rush the start of the day, thinking only of the present moment and the moments to come. We forget where we are in the broader story of God's creation and redemption of the world. As you read these lines, meditate upon them. Saying this prayer day by day might do something to soften your heart.

The morning prayer is written by Greg, a financial portfolio manager and modern art collector. He has served as an elder and as a Community Group leader at Redeemer.

"I'm from the Midwest but have been in New York City since 1971, with a 12-year hiatus in Colorado. My first prayer was alone, at night, in a car, driving through Illinois cornfields to win a client account."

But You, O LORD are a shield about me, my glory, and the One who lifts my head.

PSALM 3:3

GOD, I PRAY TO YOU through the privilege gained for me by your Son. You went from being creator to creature and chose to come as a creature of low estate. You left the perfect harmony of heaven to undertake our circumstances in a world broken by sin. Jesus, you stepped into my place, and on the cross, you took on my sin. You endured the wrath of our Father against my sin, suffered the loss of hope as you entered the crushing blackness and emptiness that is existence without him. You credited me with your goodness, making me acceptable to our Father. May I look upon the price you paid, and be sobered.

May I remember that you had to pursue me and subdue me with this gift and may it lead me to be open and hopeful for others. May I bear witness to the hope that I have in the total assurance of complete grace and infinite love through you. I pray that I would look at the price you paid and the blessing that you bestowed and that it would be my foundation, shaping my reactions to all circumstances, informing my expectations, anchoring my reality and self-worth.

Father, I pray to you along with the Holy Spirit, who prays wisely and completely for me. I thank you for choosing me and enabling me to see the truth about my Father, my Savior, and you. I pray that I

would see my gifts clearly and use them in complete harmony with my Father's purposes and that I would not shrink back or be entitled or lazy in their use. I pray that I would not grieve your Spirit; that I would not make sin my goal, planning for it and striving toward it. I pray that I would more fully experience and exhibit your fruit, especially love; that I would love as I have been loved, that I would see how esteemed I am in your love that I could never feel truly threatened. I pray that I would not sully this love with impatience, unkindness, or harshness. I ask that I would gain in faith, that I would have self-control, and that I would be good.

Father, I pray to you, the all-powerful, all-knowing, ever-present, unchangeable God. You are the creator, controller, planner, and giver of all things. You spoke all things into being, and your thoughts hold it all together. Your glory is so great it could extinguish me. Yet, you have labeled the hairs on my head. Yet, you counsel me and guide me. Yet, you shepherd and redeem me. You are a rock that I can build upon, a fortress around me, and a shield before me. May I see you in the details of my life today. May I glorify you, bear witness to my Savior, and be filled with the Holy Spirit in my thoughts, words, and deeds today.

In Jesus' name, Amen.

SECOND DAY
EVENING

At the end of the day, in the quiet of the evening, we may engage in a mental review of the day's events and our reactions and thereby conduct a self-examination of conscience and character. Did we speak, listen, do, serve, and love as we ought? The *examen* is an ancient practice of prayer in which we ask ourselves the probing questions and seek to honestly assess how we did. The goal is not to draw us to despair, but through confession, to draw us in to the peace and restfulness of experiencing the forgiveness of God.

The evening prayer is written by Leah, who, though she left her native Houston in 1999, still cherishes Texas wildflowers, huge blue skies, and barbecue. Leah moved to New York City in 2007 and started attending Redeemer in 2008. A freelance writer, musician, and arts administrator, she is also a full-time mom to two kids who spends most of her days singing kids' songs and dancing in the living room.

"I became a Christian in 1998 when I was 18 years old. What does it mean to 'truly' pray? I remember praying when I was little every time our plane to visit Grandma took off, and praying every night before bed. My understanding of God might not have been particularly robust, but those were real prayers."

But he said to me, "My grace is sufficient for you, for my power is made perfect in weakness." Therefore I will boast all the more gladly about my weaknesses, so that Christ's power may rest on me.

2 CORINTHIANS 12:9

HEAVENLY FATHER, THANK YOU for your amazing, boundless, unmerited grace. I often feel like a failure. I often feel like I have failed my family in decisions I have made, in things that I have done, and in things I have left undone. I fail them in the smallest and most unimportant ways, like when I forget to buy milk, and I fail them in much worse ways—losing my temper, intentionally blaming them for things that are my fault. The weight of my shame rests heavily on my shoulders, O God. My heart aches and longs for a way to right the wrong and earn back their love.

But I can't earn their love. I can only ask to be forgiven.

I pray for all mothers and fathers—that they would be wise, patient, and kind in the words they share with their children. I pray for orphans who have only the empty moments that the words of their parents could fill.

You loved me before I could do anything to love you back. You loved me before I had the chance to ask. You loved me before I even knew you.

I feel weak and helpless in my failings.

Your power is made perfect in my weakness. Your grace is enough for me. You redeem my failings and short-comings. It is through this that you are glorified. When I am weak and rely on you, you are glorified. When I come to the end of myself and cry out in frustration and shame, you are strong. And your grace is enough to cover over my sin when I repent and ask for forgiveness.

Father, I don't deserve this kind of unmerited kindness. Teach me how to submit to your will and help me draw near to you, especially in moments of weakness and temptation. Thank you for your astonishing grace and mercy, and for your overwhelming love. Help me to love you more, to seek you more, to worship you more.

In the name of your precious and only Son, Jesus, I pray. Amen.

THIRD DAY
MORNING

Like many New Yorkers, this writer admits she is a skeptic by nature and in this prayer reminds herself, and us, that God is greater than our hearts, and greater even than our doubts. Note her earthy sense of humor, referring to her grapefruit-sized brain and fish-like attempts at understanding. She exhibits a family-like intimacy and a natural way of confessing that sounds more like a conversation with a friend than a stiff, formal process. It is the kind of prayer written by someone who felt, even as a small child, "that I could talk to God whenever I wanted and that he would listen to anything I told him."

The morning prayer is written by Katy, who grew up in a small town in Mississippi, but moved to Romania with her missionary parents during high school. After college, she moved to New York and is now a graduate student, writer, and nanny.

"I cannot say when I became a Christian—I grew up in a family where I heard Jesus' name spoken in my home for as long as I can remember, and though I have moved through seasons of varying degrees of unbelief, I have experienced God's relentless pursuit of me, drawing me back to him over and over again. The first prayer I remember praying was thanking him for a neon green lizard I caught in our backyard one morning."

For whenever our heart condemns us,
God is greater than our hearts...

1 JOHN 3:20

FATHER,
Thank you for the assurance that you are greater than my heart, wider than the boundaries of my wandering, and deeper than my doubts.

Father, my faith is fickle. Thank you for never wavering along with the oscillating quality of my faith that can burn like fire on a Monday and is barely perceptible on a Tuesday. You know I am a doubter, a skeptic by nature. Help me to learn to doubt my doubts and fix my eyes on Jesus' empty tomb, the ultimate guarantee that you are a God who keeps your word.

Father, I understand that you are an infinite being who could not possibly fit into my grapefruit-sized brain. I know that to attempt to reduce you to something I can fully make sense of is not only arrogant but foolish, since the inchoate knowledge I have accumulated from a few decades of living has only produced fledgling ideas of your nature, and my efforts to "understand" you are as likely to succeed as a fish's attempts to "understand" the sea.

Thank you for your rhythms of grace that are as natural and inevitable as the sun rising and setting each day. Thank you that I have no more of a hand in the constancy of your character than I do in the patterns of the sun, that I have no need to beg you to be a faithful God of justice and mercy, any more than I need to implore the sun to rise each morning. As the sun rises outside my window, I long to sense the warmth of your presence the way I can feel the sun's rays and see them spilling onto my floor like golden paint.

Please fill my heart with your warmth. Illuminate the dark corners of my heart so I might shine with your light, spilling it forth wherever I find myself today. Enlighten the journalists and creative writers of this city to tell stories in line with your Story.

I pray these things in the precious and holy name of Jesus, the light of the world. Amen.

THIRD DAY
EVENING

As the writer of this prayer discovered, sometimes we work in response to God's call only to find that he has already done the work. This is, in essence, the message of the gospel—that the Son of God has already done the work we could never do. Ours is only to respond in gratitude and obedience, bringing this good news on the mountain and wherever we go.

The evening prayer is written by Jeff, a manager at a large credit-card company. Jeff was raised in California and became a Christian while in college there. He joined Redeemer when he moved to New York. The first time he ever prayed was with the people who shared the gospel with him.

"The first time I heard the gospel, I believed. I was led in a prayer of faith. I was a sophomore at college and it was after a lengthy dinner on a school night. But it didn't matter, because I had finally met my Creator."

How beautiful on the mountains are the feet of those who bring good news, who proclaim peace, who bring good tidings, who proclaim salvation, who say to Zion, "Your God reigns!"

ISAIAH 52:7

HEAVENLY FATHER, you promised freedom through redemption, so we prepared for the Redeemer. You commanded the discipling of all nations, so we prepared for the nations. But you warned love would grow cold, so we prepared for the cold.

When we went searching, behold, you had already given the Redeemer—he is Christ the King, king of kings, and he is redeeming, and we have been redeemed.

When we went searching, behold, the nations had already come—this is New York City, city of cities, and every nation, tribe, people, and tongue are here.

When we went searching, behold, love had already grown cold—these are the last days, woe of woes, and love is no more.

The times are dark and cold, and everyone does what is right in his own eyes. But for every season of pain and suffering, there is a glimmer of hope. Let truth be the light in darkness and love the warmth in cold. Who have the nations to turn to but Jesus Christ the Redeemer?

In our consumer culture, we spend so much time swiping and clicking and getting what we want with the stroke of a pen. It is easy to treat your grace cheaply too. Help us, Lord, to see the cost of discipleship.

Make us like your *prophets*, who spoke the truth and called people to repent.

Make us like your *priests*, who served in the temple and called people to worship.

Make us like your *apostles*, who founded the church and called people to enter.

Make us like your *disciples*, who lived together and called people to obedience.

Make us like your *Son*, who died for the world and called people to him.

The people of our city—each of them has a story, a story that matters to you, and we want you to be written into every one of them. I pray for our church. I pray for this city. I pray for the world. I ask these things to the glory of your name.

Amen.

FOURTH DAY
MORNING

In this prayer, the writer addresses the needs of the marginalized in our city. It is easy to walk by, to do nothing, to continue along the Jericho road. It is harder to help, to know what to do.

The morning prayer is written by Esther, a director at Hope for New York, an organization that works with Redeemer and other churches in New York to direct volunteers and donations to some of the most effective social services organizations in the city. Originally from Phoenix, Arizona, Esther has been in New York City since 2005, living in the financial district.

"I became a Christian when I was five years old, but the gospel became more real to me while I was in college. Besides blessing the food at the family dinner table, the first 'true' prayer I remember was with my Mom; I asked her about what it meant to ask Jesus in my heart (I heard my Grandfather ask me that) and she helped me pray to accept Jesus as Savior."

And Abraham called the name of that place Jehovah Jireh:
as it is said to this day, In the mount of the LORD it shall be seen.

GENESIS 22:14

LORD, I THANK YOU that you are a God of mercy, of deep compassion, and of generous justice. You are the Great Creator. You have made this world and all that is in it. Thank you that I can come before you as your child, because of the sacrifice of the perfect Lamb of God, Jesus. I worship you and praise your holy name.

Lord, I confess my own brokenness and rebellion. Each morning I set out to live rightly. But each evening, if I am honest, there are many examples of ways I have again failed. I confess my selfishness, my bitterness, and my apathy towards others and towards you. I pray for the forgiveness of my sins. Create in me a clean heart, O God, and renew a right spirit within me.

As I come to you, I humbly remember that you are God and I am not. You are at work in my life, in the life of those around me, and all around this city. Give me your eyes and your heart as I go about my day. Remove the callousness of my heart and remind me of your purpose for my presence here on earth "for such a time as this."

Lord, thank you for your promise that if I confess my sins, you are faithful and just to forgive my sins and to cleanse me from all unrighteousness.

Thank you for being the Lord of this city and Lord of my life. I trust that you are at work in my community, in my home, in my family, and in my workplace, and that you bring about renewal, healing, and flourishing.

Thank you that I can be part of your renewal here on earth. In your renewing work, help me to know how to befriend the lonely, to love those with little voice. Help me to know what it means to gracefully and humbly extend "a cup of cold water in your name."

I pray for the brokenhearted, that you would reveal yourself as the Restorer; for those who struggle with addiction, that you would show yourself as the God who "sets the captive free;" for those without work or who struggle in their work, that you would show yourself as Jehovah Jireh, "the Lord who provides;" for those with physical ailments, that you would show yourself as Healer; for all of us, that you would show yourself as Savior.

May your church be known as a people who love you, serve you, and work towards healing and renewal in every way. May the church be marked by your generous justice and deep mercy, Jesus. I give you all these prayers and lift them up to you.

In Jesus' name, Amen.

FOURTH DAY
EVENING

This prayer opens with the word "Hosanna," which means, roughly, "Save us, we pray." The word is used as an expression of joy and praise because the request has already been granted: We are saved. In this prayer, the writer deals with the topic of adversity, trials, and hardship. The scriptures teach over and over that God in his wisdom allows his children to face these troubles for various reasons and disciplines and chastens the ones he loves. The writer admits how easily he forgets this and how much he would rather seek comfort than to learn the difficult lessons of hardship. How many of us would say the same?

The evening prayer is written by Ryan, who works at one of the world's largest financial asset management firms in a group responsible for investing money on behalf of governments. He was born and raised in Dallas and started attending Redeemer when he moved to New York City.

"I became a Christian when I was five years old but have spent the last 20 years realizing what that actually means and how wonderful of a thing it is. The first prayers that I remember praying by myself were in elementary school. I would pray for two things—that everyone in the world who God was calling would become a Christian and that I wouldn't have any nightmares or bad dreams."

*...the Lord disciplines those he loves and
he chastens everyone he accepts as his son.*

HEBREWS 12:6

HOSANNA! HOSANNA TO MY GOD, the one who has delivered me. You provided for me before I knew you and you claimed me as your son. What wonderful truth is this that you would consider a wretch like me worthy of adoption as your child? While I cannot fully understand this, I can look to the incarnation of this love in the person of Jesus Christ, your one true Son. I praise you now, Jesus, my good friend, because whereas I distrusted the Father's goodness, you loved him perfectly to the point of submitting to death and eternal isolation, all for our sake! Oh Jesus, you are greater than all men. You are perfectly God!

And I am not.

I admit I don't endure hardship as discipline and forget these words of encouragement you have given your children: *The Lord disciplines those he loves and he chastens everyone he accepts as a son.* I confess that I deflect hardship for the sake of comfort and when by your grace you put your heavy hand of discipline on me, I despair and grumble. I'm sorry, Lord! Were I to really understand what you've done for me, I would undertake any hardship.

Lord, how could it be that some are so wealthy while others barely have enough to eat? May those who are making decisions about where to invest huge pools of capital remember there are many tonight with no money at all. I pray that our times would be marked by greater justice, greater mercy, and greater generosity.

Thank you, Jesus, for taking on the burden and heartbreak so that I, along with all our brothers and sisters, can experience the holiness of God and inherit his kingdom. And Lord, usher in your kingdom! Especially today, grant perseverance to your servants who are being persecuted for proclaiming the name of your Son. Let them fix their eyes on Jesus, who for the joy set before him scorned the shame of ultimate persecution on the cross.

In their hardship, in my hardship, and in every hardship we are all sure to face, let us identify with Christ as fellow heirs and as sons of the Father. Let your kingdom come in the name of the Father, the Son, and the Holy Spirit.

Amen.

Hebrews 12:6

FIFTH DAY
MORNING

The writers of this morning prayer know how easy it can be to go through this city of "extremes" and not see God at work. New York has more billionaires than any city in the world—yet the problem of homelessness feels intractable, with nearly 60,000 living on the streets. Before the writers begin their day in the most densely populated city in America, they pray to remember that every single person they come in contact with is an image-bearer of God.

The morning prayer is written by Greg and Ashley, who met in New York City while attending Redeemer. They are now married and raising two children downtown. Greg, a Pittsburgh native, is an investor and serves as a deacon. Hailing from Dallas, Ashley works as a counselor with Redeemer Counseling Services. They both co-lead a Community Group. Greg and Ashley both started attending Redeemer during Redeemer's 2005 Vision Campaign.

"For both of us, our first prayer was asking Jesus to be Lord of our lives. For Greg, that was in college, and, for Ashley, that was in second grade."

Then God said, "Let us make man in our image, in our likeness, and let them rule over the fish of the sea and the birds of the air, over the livestock, over all the earth, and over all the creatures that move along the ground." So God created man in his own image, in the image of God he created him; male and female he created them.

GENESIS 1:26–27

DEAR HEAVENLY FATHER, It can be so easy to go through this city of "extremes" and not see God at work. Within the same few square miles live multi-millionaires and yet also thousands of people who have no home. The Bible affirms that all men and women are created in your likeness. We praise you for this truth—that you made us, and we are equally precious to you. We ask this morning that we might see everyone in this city as an image-bearer of yours.

We understand the gospel is meant to change all areas of our lives. God help us to see your creation more like Jesus.

As we ride a crowded train in the city... let us see people as you see them.

As we navigate crowds at rush hour... let us see people as you see them.

As we interact at work, with our bosses, with our clients, with our peers... let us see people as you see them.

Please help me to embrace this place I call home.

There's more beauty on those subway rides than in our renowned museums, as each of us is your masterpiece. Give me a caring heart for those with mental illness, those on the streets each day, and those looking for work. Ultimately, may your Holy Spirit encourage us not to be impatient and short with others, but to take this city's density and diversity as an opportunity to live out the gospel, and to see in every face the reflected glory of the face who made them.

FIFTH DAY
EVENING

The writer of this prayer, a litigator, says her work often involves evidence, advocacy, and the binding power of words. She says these things have a strong influence on her prayer life as well. Note how she returns again and again to the promises in God's Word. Her prayer is rooted in the Word of God. Her words arise as a response to his first word.

The evening prayer is written by Katie, who has lived in New York City since 2005 and attended Redeemer since 2012. She has also lived in upstate New York, Virginia, California, and the U.K. She became a Christian at age 15, after a close friend shared the gospel with her. She volunteers on the communion team at church and at a soup kitchen on the Lower East Side.

"When I was a new Christian, my pastor canceled the sermon he had prepared one Sunday morning so we could pray for a little girl in our congregation who was on the brink of death from a sudden virus. The doctors had given up. She lived. It changed me forever."

May God be gracious to us and bless us and make his face shine on us—
so that your ways may be known on earth, your salvation among all nations.

PSALM 67:1–2

FATHER, your Word says: *"The king-dom of God is not a matter of talk but of power."*

So I'm asking for demonstrations of the power of the Holy Spirit in your church. We struggle to trust you to exercise power in our lives, but on the cross you proved yourself infinitely trustworthy. We are the ones who often prove un-trustworthy stewards.

Your Word says: *"The appetite of labor-ers works for them, drives them on."*

Fill us, your servants, with a driving hunger to see our lives electrified by the power of your presence in us. Make us long to radiate with the wonders of your great love. Ignite in us the desire to love others with your wisdom, power, and steadfast determination. Forgive our mistrust of you, and make us trustworthy stewards of the power of your Holy Spirit. Exercise such power in us that we are living proof of your mercy, and let us participate as you help others in astonishing ways.

Your Word says: *"Do not let the oppressed retreat in disgrace; may the poor and needy praise your name."*

Alert us to their needs and teach us to pray courageously for them. Answer our prayers so profoundly that the only credible explanation is the work of our loving and almighty Father. Who else could do this? Who else would?

Your Word says: *"Whoever believes in Jesus will do even greater things than he did."*

Empower us through prayer to heal the sick, correct injustice, and bear your light in darkness. Send us out to feed the hungry in our city; be glorified as you restore their hope and dignity. Father, choose us to help unburden those who are crushed under the weight of shame and unmet expectations. Appoint us to untie those bound by sin and death with the good news of freedom in Christ. Use us to bring fresh evidence of your mercy to light, and advance your gospel into new hearts. Teach us to delight in all these blessings and in the treasure of knowing you in Christ.

I ask in the name you gave us, Jesus Christ.

1 Corinthians 4:20, Proverbs 16:26, Psalm 74:21, John 14:12

SIXTH DAY
MORNING

The nature of this life is that we are regularly sailing through storms. As we are tossed by the waves, it is tempting to lose perspective and hope. This writer begins her prayer in praise of God's love, and the power of his word to calm the storms. She goes on to confess a weakness of faith, then moves boldly to ask God's blessing on families.

～

The morning prayer is written by Ellen, currently a stay-at-home mother. Born in Ethiopia, Ellen became a Christian "gradually but officially at age eight." She moved to New York in 1988 and has been at Redeemer since 1994.

"When I was seven years old, I went to boarding school. There, my homesickness drove me to pray. I would try to replicate my parents' prayers, but I would also pour my heart out and ask God to be with me. And he was."

The disciples went and woke him, saying, "Master, Master, we're going to drown!" He got up and rebuked the wind and the raging waters; the storm subsided, and all was calm.

LUKE 8:24

HEAVENLY FATHER, I praise you for your fatherly love that knows no end, for your peace that passes all understanding, for your power that stills the violent storms of nature with a word, and that can still the violent storms of our hearts with a sigh.

My heart wrestles between the anger of not getting my way and the guilt of knowing it's all idol worship. I misconstrue the desires of my heart as being your will. And yet, when I seek you, I find you. Your promise to never leave or forsake me remains fast. Your unwillingness to give up on me astounds me and fills my heart with gratitude. Your care extends to every person on this earth. Let that soften my heart and challenge me to love them as you do, to lift them up for your glory.

I pray:

For the families you have formed; that you would bring guidance to those couples who attempt to live out their marriages in godly reflection; that they love each other as you model, not as the world pressures; that they would learn the deep joy of sacrificial love and steadfast commitment.

For those who long for marriage, who feel the pangs of loneliness and self-doubt, Lord Jesus, bring confidence in your delight in them, that they would rejoice in the knowledge that you are the love they long for and that your plans for their lives while they wait are perfectly planned and God-breathed.

For parents struggling to raise their children to glorify and enjoy you forever, give patience and understanding for their children who are swimming against the tide of the world's pull. Give them courage and perseverance in teaching their children your truths. Fill them with the peace that you, Lord, are our true Father and that their children are secure in your arms.

For the elderly, bring comfort. To those with no means, Lord, convict us to care for their needs. For those who are isolated and lonely, bring into their lives people who would reflect your peace and encouragement, who would remind them that despite our culture's tendency to neglect them, they are of utmost value to you, who loves them.

Heavenly Father, thank you that your love and compassion is for every last one of your children. You are our Father, our Savior, our Lord.

In Jesus' name, Amen.

SIXTH DAY
EVENING

This writer fills her prayer with praise for God. For many of us, it is too easy to skip past appreciating God and move immediately on to listing what we want and think we need. We act like self-centered children, constantly nagging their parents for candy. Note the writer's points of emphasis, illustrated with italics and exclamation points, and her exuberant tone. She is awed and amazed by God's gift to her—the same gift he has bestowed on all of us. This prayer is a reminder of the opportunity to live a God-centered life.

The evening prayer is written by Rose-Marie, a writer, seminary graduate, retired public affairs specialist, and entrepreneur. She was born in New York and raised in a Christian home. Having been "born anew" in her early fifties, Rose-Marie has been at Redeemer since 2005.

"My first prayer was The Lord's Prayer—very seriously at about four years old. Prayer for me is like food—it is impossible for me to live without it."

I am the way and the truth and the life.
No one comes to the Father except through me.

JOHN 14:6

DEAR GOD the Father, God the Son, God the Holy Spirit, Almighty God. You are the maker of heaven and earth and all that is in them, creator of every created thing. You are the one who gives the breath of life.

And yet you tell me I can call you *Abba*, Father. And yet you know my name. You know *my* name! I want to magnify you with my every thought. I want to praise you with every breath. I want to thank you for every indescribable gift of your love, through Christ Jesus my Lord!

Heavenly Father, your praises are continually in my mouth. You became poor that I might become rich, that I might know the depth of the riches of your grace. You made yourself lost that I might be found, that I might enter into the way, the truth, and the life.

Who am I, Lord God, that you sacrificed your son—yourself!—to offer me eternal life? I have the privilege now of dwelling forever with the whole fullness of the Godhead—Father, Son, and Holy Spirit. How can I ever praise you enough for this gift of a love that is greater than life, a love that transcends life? By dying on the cross, dear Jesus, you turned death into life for *me* and for all who will believe. While I was still your enemy, you loved me.

Teach me this love so I can understand what it means to love my neighbor as myself—to lay down my life for others. This is the kind of love you said equals all the law and the prophets.

Lord, cleanse me with hyssop, wash me that I may be whiter than snow, create in me a pure heart and a right spirit so that I can be an example of your perfect love.

This is my prayer, *Abba*, Father: I pray for a heart sanctified by Christ-like love from which I will lift up my praises to you, honor you, and glorify your name.

Matthew 22:40, Psalm 51

SEVENTH DAY
MORNING

The author of this prayer reverses the way we typically think about money by declaring right from the start that none of it is ours; it all belongs to the Lord. From that perspective, he offers this prayer asking for wisdom on how to spend and invest and share our money well.

⁓

The morning prayer is written by Patrick, who is originally from College Station, Texas. Formerly a professional tennis player, Patrick spent a year at the Trinity Forum Academy and two years in business school to transition into a career in philanthropic advising, helping donors flourish. In 2014, he moved to New York and began attending Redeemer. He is part of the 2015-16 Gotham Fellows class.

"The first prayer I remember praying was as an un-churched 17-year-old responding to a youth leader's call to follow Christ after wrestling with and being captivated by Christ's claims, actions, and character."

Yours, O LORD, is the greatness and the power and the glory and the victory
and the majesty, for all that is in the heavens and in the earth is yours.
Yours is the kingdom, O LORD, and you are exalted as head above all.
Both riches and honor come from you, and you rule over all. In your hand
are power and might, and in your hand it is to make great and to give strength
to all. And now we thank you, our God, and praise your glorious name.

1 CHRONICLES 29:11–13

LORD, YOU ARE THE OWNER OF everything that is. Even more than that, you are the active agent in anything that is good. Tempted to believe that I am ultimately in control of my financial situation, I desperately need this reminder. Lord, help me be sober-minded in plenty and in want, honoring you as the source of all provision and leading me to worship.

As I move into my daily routine, I face such an abundance of financial choices: the allure of endless comforts, the needs all around me, and the balance of personal savings. Help me navigate your call to save wisely, to give sacrificially, to invest shrewdly, and to celebrate extravagantly.

Lord, draw near to me that I might hear your voice while approaching these decisions with open hands. Call me into the deep waters—where the rich young ruler is invited to give all he has, where Mary is invited to lavish Jesus with perfume, and where the owners of talents are to dutifully seek a proper return.

Bring financial freedom where my bank account mirrors the gospel: "It is for freedom that Christ had set us free."

Lord, help me set my hope on you and take hold of true life, according to 1 Timothy 6:17:

"As for the rich in this present age, charge them not to be haughty, nor to set their hopes on the uncertainty of riches, but on God, who richly provides us with everything to enjoy. They are to do good, to be rich in good works, to be generous and ready to share, thus storing up treasure for themselves as a good foundation for the future, so that they may take hold of that which is truly life."

Lord, you say that where my treasure is, there my heart will be also. Have your way with my finances that my heart may be fully yours.

Amen.

SEVENTH DAY
EVENING

In this prayer, the writer describes the struggle of the Christian life, where we repeatedly turn from God, and to him, and from him again in sequence. She describes herself as two persons: the one who loves God, and the one who is continually distracted by daily life. Many of us can relate to that tension. And yet each time we turn away, we look back and find God waiting patiently with open arms.

☙

The evening prayer is written by Hally, a policy analyst working in the office of the Manhattan borough president. She has been a New Yorker for 12 years, an East Harlemite for seven, and has attended Redeemer since the mid-2000s. She has at various points called Hong Kong, Seattle, Los Angeles, central Jersey, and upstate New York "home."

"While my parents were not themselves believers, they were the first to expose me to Christianity, enrolling me in an Anglican primary school. Later, in an effort to retain my knowledge of Chinese after I immigrated to the U.S., my dad subscribed me to a Christian Chinese magazine. Everything eventually started to make sense and at 14, I became a Christian.

Some of my first communications with God were saying 'Not yet' or 'Let me think about it' when he first started to call me. It was summer vacation at Grandma's. I had a lot of time to think—and by extension, to make excuses—before finally surrendering."

Whoever wants to be my disciple must deny
themselves and take up their cross daily and follow me.

LUKE 9:23

M Y SOUL cries out to you, O God.
In the morning, in that
suspended instant when
darkness meets first light—
When I am on the cusp of
consciousness and know
I am still sleeping,
In limbo between dreaming
and waking—
I exist only for you.
How long have I been crying out,
Words flowing from the depths
of my heart to my Savior?
I need you, I say, *I yearn for you.*
I love you.
Then I open my eyes.
Instead of beholding your beauty,
I become captivated by my iDevice.
Instead of delighting in your Word,
my eyes glaze over as I compose my
mental to-do list.
Instead of walking with you,
I rush out the door.
And instead of listening,
I have become deaf to the pleas
of those around me:
"Quarter, penny, nickel, dime,
Can anybody help?"
Why am I two persons,
one who loves you and one who
lives as though you do not exist?
You call me to bring your light to the
city, to lift up those bowed down
with life's burdens,

To advocate for those caught on
the wrong side of inequality.
How can I do this, when by day
my heart is far from you?
Feed the hungry. Free prisoners
from the shackles of their past.
Empower people to live in dignity.
I pray for the leaders
and policy makers of our city.
Give them wisdom and courage
to decide rightly.
But it is not just the officials
who should act.
I should too.
So I take steps forward, put my hands
to the task... I can do it myself, I think.
I exhaust my last drop of strength
until nothing is left.
But you hold me still.
When I lift my eyes, you are there.
You are the hope for this world,
this city. *Follow me*, you say—
It has always been your one
and only call.
O Lord, I will follow you.
Then you will establish the works
of my hands. You will draw me
to yourself and never let me go.
O Lord, do not let go.
Let me be where you are.
Let me praise you in work and in rest,
Let me say to you with all my heart:
I need you.
I yearn for you.
I love you.

EIGHTH DAY
MORNING

The writer of this prayer gives voice to those who are faced with a time of frustration and change at work. She begins by confessing to God her desire for relief from her own situation, going on to acknowledge that she only need trust in him to experience peace—even if circumstances do not change. She ends with a humble request that she herself could be an emissary of God's comfort for those with whom she works.

~~

The morning prayer is written by Lourine, an executive coach and transplant from the Midwest who has had deep roots in New York for more than 30 years. When she first visited the city in her mid-twenties, she realized "about two minutes into the taxi ride from the airport" that she would have to live here someday. She and her husband, Greg, have been at Redeemer since 2002, after living off of Redeemer sermon CDs during their "wilderness years" in Colorado.

"I became a believer through the faithful prayers of our housekeeper, who never spoke a word to Greg or me, but spoke plenty to God about us! My first real prayer was one year after conversion. I was in my mid-thirties and had just been told by my organization that I had a new role. But I was planning my exit! I realized I had never prayed about work before, and it was time to start."

This is what the Lord says: "Stand at the crossroads
and look; ask for the ancient paths, ask where the good way is,
and walk in it, and you will find rest for your souls."

JEREMIAH 6:16A

GRACIOUS FATHER, thank you that you invite your children to come to you with confidence, that you will not turn us away in our time of need. I want to thank you for how, when I am stressed with work, I am reminded of my deep need to depend upon you instead of myself. When I am exhausted and afraid, I know I am depending on myself and not you! Lord, have mercy on me.

Your Word says we can count our trials as joy because you promise to use them to shape us into the image of your Son. You promise also to give me wisdom for all sorts of trials if I will but come to you in faith—trusting that you will guide me if I come wanting your will above my own. But I confess that right now I just want out of the trials.

Forgive me for this way of approaching you, asking you to do my will. Grant me a heart and mind that truly wants your way instead of my own. Grant me a growing trust in you and a belief that what you desire for me is good because you are good. Grant in me a desire to let you use this crossroads at work to change me, to heal me of leaning on my own understanding rather than yours.

Thank you that your Word gives instruction in "crossroads." Help me to be still enough to stand in the crossroads instead of running around, asking everyone for advice except you. Help me to quiet myself so you can show me the "ancient paths." You are working things out for good. I ask that you would teach me how I need to change in this whole mess—how to listen to you more keenly so I will walk on your good way.

Father, teach me not to lean on my own understanding, to acknowledge you in all my ways and to trust in you with all of my heart. Already my soul is coming to rest, even though my circumstances haven't changed. Help me also, I pray, to be an encouragement to the people around me at work who are also struggling. Let me be an encourager of them, a light in a dark place. Let my words be helpful for building them up. Let me not fall into the temptation of complaining. Use me, I pray.

With gratitude I pray these things in Jesus's name, Amen.

Hebrews 4:16, James 1:2-8, Psalm 46:10, Romans 8:28, Psalm 131, Proverbs 3:5-6, Ephesians 4:29

EIGHTH DAY
EVENING

The writer of this prayer offers a poignant and personal confession of the bitterness she sometimes feels inside. She fears not receiving praise, and not being remembered. So caught up in her own search for the admiration of others, she sometimes forgets the love of God entirely. One of the hard-fought points of spiritual maturity is learning how to not chase the affirmation of the crowds and instead feel the affirmation of the maker of the clouds.

The evening prayer is written by Rachel, a recent New York transplant who is originally from Tennessee. Rachel and her husband are both composers and have a grey housecat named Haydn. She became a Christian as a young teenager and began attending Redeemer in 2013.

"I think the first time I truly prayed was in a group in my late twenties. I had a pastor who really emphasized the importance of prayer, of praying through scripture, and of praying in a community. Those Wednesday night prayer meetings had quite an effect on me."

He was despised and rejected by mankind, a man of suffering,
and familiar with pain. Like one from whom people hide their faces
he was despised, and we held him in low esteem.

ISAIAH 53:3

FATHER, I AM NOT CONTENT. More than I'd like to admit, I feel you are not enough. Sometimes I love music more than I love you. I write for my own glory, to be praised for my genius, to be counted among the great. In my quest to be remembered, I forget you.

And yet my art is a poor reflection of your beauty. Whatever genius I sometimes think I have is not my own. There is nothing new under the sun. I am not original and I know it.

Each success is fleeting. Each failure chips away pieces of my heart. I struggle beneath the weight of proving myself over and over. I feel like an imposter, a fake. I always fear that I will be found out. I live in fear of rejection and in fear of success. How will I outdo what I have already done? What will I do if my work isn't good enough?

Am I not good enough?

Forgive me: I avoid my fellow creators. I cannot enjoy their happiness. I am envious of their success. I constantly compare my work to their work, plotting their failure in my heart, fearful their work will be praised and loved and mine will be forgotten.

You were rejected; you were despised. You gave up your own glory for me. I live as if I don't care, clutching at the approval of other people and holding tightly to my need to be loved and admired for my ability. Convince my heart of your never ending, always love. Remind me daily that you are the source of my creativity; you are the only truly original Creator. Capture my heart with your beauty. Help me to measure my worth by your Word. Satisfy my soul with your presence. Teach me to order my loves; you first, you only. For only then will I be content in you.

I pray Lord that the concert halls would be filled with sounds of glory and that those who hear the music would recognize a beauty beyond the beauty of the song. I ask it in Jesus' name, Amen.

NINTH DAY
MORNING

This writer prays for those who are lost. Through parables, Jesus describes his heavenly Father as the kind of God who, like a shepherd searches for the lost sheep, like an old woman searches for a lost coin, and like a concerned father welcomes back his lost son. He is not indifferent. He is a God on mission for those he loves and he promises not to let his loved ones go.

❧

The morning prayer is written by Sharon, who lives in New Jersey and leads a Community Group of Redeemer women that meets in her home. Raised by Christian parents, she moved to Japan with her husband and lived there for 14 years before moving back to the U.S. She has been attending Redeemer for about 10 years.

"Since coming to Redeemer, I have had an increasing desire to pray, realizing what I needed more than anything else was intimacy with God. I have found that in prayer increasingly, for which I am very thankful. I have a long way to go still, but God is so gracious in meeting me with his love.

I remember being in my bedroom with my mother and asking Jesus to come into my heart, and thanking him for being my Savior. Probably something like, 'Dear Lord Jesus, thank you for dying on the cross for me. Please come into my heart and live there. Amen.' I must have been around six years old."

The Lord is gracious and compassionate,
slow to anger and rich in love.

PSALM 145:8

HEAVENLY FATHER, I THANK YOU that you are a God who keeps your promises. And because of Jesus Christ I can come to you with my prayers for those I love who have turned from you. Your covenant love and faithfulness seen throughout the scriptures give me great hope to come to you boldly.

Thank you that love is at the center of all your attributes, and you yourself tell us, if you did not spare your only Son, but gave him up for us all, how will you not freely along with him graciously give us all things? Father, because you have already done that unimaginably hard thing with your most beloved, now please give my loved ones the gift of your Holy Spirit, bringing conviction, repentance, and faith in your Son. I especially pray for _____.

You have made my loved ones, and they are yours. You have blessed them with your goodness in so many ways—please do not give them these many good gifts without giving them yourself. Show them you have not forgotten or abandoned them.

Remember you are a merciful God. Remember this is why you sent Jesus: for people like us. Remember Jesus could not be parted from his people and so he died for us, making atonement, and is interceding for us at this moment. I join my prayers with him, and stand beside my loved ones, pleading your mercy.

Father, forgive me when I have allowed their salvation to become my hope, instead of you, my covenant-keeping God, my sovereign King, my Savior. You alone are the Lord of Salvation. Keep my eyes fixed on you. For your name's sake, redeem us because of your unfailing, unconditional, covenant love by which you have obligated yourself to your people, just as you did with the Israelites of old. You have paid the infinitely costly price to do that, for which I thank you with all my heart. Thank you for hearing my prayers. Bring glory to Jesus, in whose name I pray, Amen.

NINTH DAY
EVENING

This evening prayer was originally written for a men's group of the church but is universal in its concerns. As you read it, do you find yourself struck by the humility of the tone and his honest confessions of his need for help? Most of us have just as many weaknesses and needs but don't often say them so plainly. This prayer is an example of the freedom to be transparent because of the gospel.

The evening prayer is written by Jerry, a long-time college administrator who has become an entrepreneur. He was born and raised in Annapolis, Maryland, moved to Seattle after high school, then to New York in 1989. He has been attending Redeemer for more than 20 years.

"I was raised in the Episcopal Church and I remember loving God since I was a boy. That said, my spiritual journey has been one of progressive revelation, accelerated when I began attending Redeemer, then thrust into high gear after getting married and becoming more active with my wife in a Beta group, West Side Catalyst, and then co-founding and leading the West Side Men's Group with a friend. As a child, my mother taught us to kneel and say our prayers before bed, including praying for our family members."

*Your people will rebuild the ancient ruins and will raise up
the age-old foundations; you will be called Repairer of Broken Walls,
Restorer of Streets with Dwellings.*

ISAIAH 58:12

BELOVED FATHER IN HEAVEN, Almighty God, thank you for your generous blessing upon our lives. May I hear your voice and reach for your calm, steady hand and know that you are where I am, working within me, bathed in your everlasting light.

As I lay awake at night or get distracted at work or close myself off at home worrying about my measure, may I remember that you sanctify me more than I understand. Remind me that, incredibly, you care about the details of my life and are there to pick me up when I fall. Lord, please give me the strength:

...to align my desires with yours so I make a difference by being different,

...to answer the calls of my brothers and sisters in need,

...to act truthfully and rid my heart of malice,

...to show others the kind of truth that frustrates the ways of the world.

Please extinguish my fear and indecision and dissolve my desire to be in the inner circles. Give me what I need in health and the health of my family so when times are tough, I may persevere against sin and be a soldier of kindness, leaving the justice to you—always remembering that sometimes the very worst things that happen can turn into the very best things, through you, Lord God.

Please forgive me for my tempted thoughts, my wayward glances, my impure deeds, seeking rewards I did not earn. Oh, the things I say, the shortsighted ways I spend my money, guard my time, and shut my doors.

Instead, may I have a heart like a child, allowing you to be the power where I work or with those I love or on the street with the strangers you place before me. With your grace living in my heart, may I act! May I shout that you, Lord, are the repairer of broken streets, the architect of all power and glory, the very essence of power in the universe.

You, Lord, have always been, are now, and forever will be there for us. Thank you. In the precious name of Jesus, I pray.

Amen.

TENTH DAY
MORNING

This writer prays for perseverance. The scriptures encourage us to consider it joy when we face hardships because they eventually produce perseverance. In New York, we say if you can make it here, you can make it anywhere—but it's awfully hard to make it here. We need hope. We need resources like rooted homes. We need each other. And we need to persevere.

～

The morning prayer is written by Bjorn, a dancer from Denmark who has been living in New York for about three years. Bjorn came from an "unbelieving" family, but remembers being interested in Christianity as a kid. He independently started to read the Bible and believe around age 12.

He discovered Redeemer in 2013 after passing by the church on West 83rd Street while on his way to the post office.

"I first prayed as I was studying the Bible, starting with the *Gospel According to Matthew*, and started joining the lunchtime prayer group at my school. As a kid, I really needed help and a sense that there was justice in life. I prayed for that."

Consider it pure joy, my brothers and sisters, whenever you face trials
of many kinds, because you know that the testing of your faith
produces perseverance. Let perseverance finish its work so that you
may be mature and complete, not lacking anything.

JAMES 1:2–4

How LONG HAVE I STRUGGLED IN your service, Lord?

How long have I held on to hopes that I haven't reached?

I know you have not forgotten about me. I look forward to finding out how I fit into your plan.

I know to persevere, and I thank you for your faithfulness.

Please forgive me if I have become distracted or lost direction at times.

Please forgive me if I have not been there for those I care about, or not been alert to opportunities to reach out to others.

I thank you for your very present power in my life that enables me to continue and be strong.

I ask you to help me in my daily tasks, to remain unpolluted by the world, unpolluted by temptations from others or my circumstances. I will seek you every day, in the mornings and in the evenings. I know you will guide me and comfort me.

I ask you to give me time, time to spend with the brothers and sisters in faith, time to build on the goals I have started on, and to see the race to completion.

I ask you to instruct me where I have fallen short, where I have not done what it takes to get the job done, or to follow your word. I love instruction and wisdom, and listen gladly.

I ask you to hold on to those of the household of faith, to watch over them always with encouragement and grant them perception, to watch over them always with healing, both physical and spiritual. And give your people homes to welcome others into, homes not for ourselves, but to be shared with our neighbors.

In Jesus' wonderful and joyous name, I pray.

Amen.

TENTH DAY
EVENING

In this end-of-day prayer, the writer asks for peace and quiet after the strain of the day, and the strain of a long season in the wilderness. There is a Lenten spirit to her prayer, an acknowledgment that the Christian life is sometimes dry, but it never remains so. We read in scripture that God allowed his people to wander in the wilderness for 40 years. They had no home and nowhere to go. But he always led them. And he leads us still.

The evening prayer is written by Pamela, who is in the business of soul care, having served as a staff leader of Community Groups for our church. She was born and raised in Nigeria, by her Nigerian father and her Northern Irish mother. She became a Christian as a teenager.

"In college, I drifted away from Jesus. When God brought me to New York 25 years ago to pursue graduate work in public health, he also brought me back to himself. After 15 years of working in AIDS, God called me to a pastoral role at Redeemer. I first attended a Redeemer service 17 years ago. I knew no one until I joined a Community Group. It changed my life (and eventually my career too)!

My first prayer was when I was 13. I sat quietly in my bedroom alone and acknowledged before God that I was a sinner and Christ died for me. Much later in my thirties, my recommitment prayer was more desperate: 'I've tried living my way; it doesn't work. God, I'm willing to try your way.'"

Whoever dwells in the shelter of the Most High will rest in the
shadow of the Almighty. I will say of the Lord,
"He is my refuge and my fortress, my God, in whom I trust."

PSALM 91:1–2

GRACIOUS FATHER IN HEAVEN, I am sighing and often lonely at the end of the day. At times you seem absent though I know you never are. You are everywhere: in every face, at every bedside, in every hospital room, in every prison cell, even at every death. Whether I'm awake or asleep, you are there. You, unlike me, never get tired or weary. You never slumber or sleep.

Yet sometimes you seem far away, as if your face is turned from me, as if you're not paying attention. You seem focused on other things, on other people perhaps. You seem hands-off, uninterested, uninvolved. Today I feel particularly concerned about _____.

Yet you whisper in my ear: "Whoever dwells in the shelter of the Most High will rest in the shadow of the Almighty." Lord, teach me what it means to dwell, to linger, to hang out, to wait for you in your secret place where you make yourself known. Help me to stick with it. Help me to stay close to you. And as I wait, show me how to slow down, how to really slow down, how not to fast-forward my day, how not to rush through life.

Show me how not to make light of these sacred moments with you even as I struggle to sense you here. Show me I'm not the only one who is tired. Help me to be your answer to someone else's prayer.

God, give me the true rest that only you can deliver. I want my soul—the deep inner places that you alone see and know and touch—to be quiet, to be still, to exhale, to trust, to be thankful, to be brave.

Fill me with hope so that I truly believe you are doing a new thing. Help me to expect it, to be patient for it, and to perceive it when it comes. And grow my faith to believe that you make a way through every wilderness.

For the glory of your name,

Amen.

ELEVENTH DAY
MORNING

This writer's prayer is what you might call other-centered or kingdom-centered prayer. He asks for nothing for himself other than for God to help him reflect heavenly kindness and care. Instead of praying for himself, he prays for the unemployed, the lonely, and those who are discriminated against, among others. May we all learn to pray like this, seeking not our own comfort, but asking instead that "thy kingdom come, thy will be done, on earth as it is in heaven."

∾

The morning prayer is written by Gary, a deacon and manager of tax processing at a "Big Four" accounting firm who rides a motorcycle in his spare time. Originally from Gordonsville, Virginia, Gary was raised a Baptist and attended several churches of other denominations after moving to New York City in 1971. He has been at Redeemer since August 2012 and is involved in several ministries.

"The earliest prayer I can remember is in my teens in the woods of Virginia on a country road, and it was essentially about desiring close friendship."

*This is what the LORD says: "Maintain justice and
do what is right, for my salvation is close at
hand and my righteousness will soon be revealed."*

ISAIAH 56:1

FATHER, I THANK YOU THAT you are sovereign and that you love us unconditionally. It is your love for us that carries me through the challenges of each day. I ask that you continue to guide and lead me even through my struggles that seem so recurrent.

I pray for those who are experiencing injustice and discrimination, that you would provide encouragement to sustain them. I pray for justice, peace, and freedom among peoples of the world, and among the neighborhoods of this city.

Help me to represent you in being reflective of your understanding and kindness. Help me to be a beacon of light and hope to my neighbors where I live, to those on the subway, and to the people I interact with daily.

I thank you for our elected government leaders, federal, state, and city, asking that you provide them with wisdom in making decisions that concern us. Please place in their hearts the desire to be sincere and honest in all their dealings.

Please give healing for those in countries where serious diseases have been discovered with no immediate cure. Protect missionaries and others who risk their lives to help those desperately in need, especially _____. I also pray for the sick and suffering, for the hungry and oppressed, and for those in prison.

Many in our congregation are unemployed or not in the job for which they are purposed. Please give them patience and trust in relying on you for a change in their status.

I pray for racial healing in our country. Bring peace and stability in cities throughout America. Please provide comfort to family and friends who are hurting. In our city, I ask that you comfort those who are lonely, that you would sustain those who are newly married, provide for those seeking to have or adopt children, and give mercy to those who are struggling with parenting.

I ask these things in the matchless name of Jesus.

Amen.

ELEVENTH DAY
EVENING

This writer begs for justice—for the poor and marginalized—and for peace among the nations of the earth. She expresses hope that one day all swords will be beaten into plowshares and that people will live in peace because someday the government will be on the shoulders of the one called the Prince of Peace. Until that day, we join the prophets in crying out for God's kingdom to come here, and soon.

The evening prayer is written by Kerri, who grew up in Los Angeles and moved to New York in 2008. She works in public relations and lives in Astoria with her husband.

"I have been at Redeemer for many years and am continually grateful for the community God has given me here. I became a Christian when I was four years old, but first came to know God's grace in a meaningful way during college. I remember praying for the first time when I was four. Praying with my mom, I told God, 'I believe in Jesus and want to be with him forever!'"

*For to us a child is born, to us a Son is given, and the government
shall be on His shoulders, and His name shall be called
Wonderful Counselor, Mighty God, Everlasting Father, Prince of Peace.*

ISAIAH 9:6

SOVEREIGN LORD OF HOPE, I see suffering, despair, and darkness around me. I am discouraged by what I see. Yet you say, "Take heart. I have overcome the world." And I remember you have not forgotten the poor, the marginalized, or the disabled. You love them beyond measure. Remind me of Jesus' humility in life and death, enabling me to serve them with generosity of prayer, time, and material goods. May the church, government, and others work together to bridge the gap between the rich and the poor and to affirm those at the fringes of society.

I see that peace eludes war-torn nations. Oppressive regimes remain in power, subjecting their people to manipulation and hardship.

Yet you have established your kingdom through Jesus Christ. Upon him and the peace he brings, "there will be no end." Your plan for redemption stands firm despite the evil that exists. Mighty God, turn the hardest of hearts toward you. Bring unjust leaders to their knees, humbled by the one true God. Raise up peacemakers and end sectarian strife. Give courage to our fellow believers in these parts of the world. Forgive us when we turn away or forget them! Teach us how to walk with them.

I see my own striving to fix the brokenness in my life. All-knowing God, you see what I do not. You see the depth of suffering, sin, and sorrow, but you also see the full plan of redemption. Because of your immeasurable grace in Jesus' death, I have hope. A hope that brings about the restoration and the wholeness of the world as you intended it be. May I cling to this truth and may people everywhere, from all walks of life, from the busiest cities to the remotest corners of the earth, know that you are the light of the world and the hope of our hearts.

Amen.

45

TWELFTH DAY
MORNING

Sometimes we think too highly of ourselves, as if the world revolved around us, as if Jesus didn't need to die for us. Other times we think too lowly of ourselves, as if Jesus weren't glad to die for us. An appropriate humility may be to see oneself as small in comparison to God's immensity and yet not ignore God's gentle eagerness to hear our prayers. This writer provides us with a wonderful example of that measured humility.

The morning prayer is written by Bob, a "semi-retired" talk-radio host who was born and raised in New York and moved back to the city to care for his mother. He grew up in a secular Jewish home but went to Trinity School and attended church at St. Bartholomew's Episcopal Church.

"I was baptized and confirmed at age 16 but later lapsed until around 30, at which time I began a passionate walk with Christ. When I was five years old, my divorced mother put me in a Catholic boarding school. When I was depressed, I went and sat alone in the chapel. I remember that empty chapel and feel sure I prayed hard."

He gathers the waters of the sea together as a heap;
He lays up the deeps in storehouses. Let all the earth fear the LORD;
Let all the inhabitants of the world stand in awe of Him.

PSALM 33:7-8

ALMIGHTY and everlasting God,
How can I pray to you?
I am so small,
So little in my understanding,
Little in all things.
But you, O God, are limitless
Beyond all things.

You alone stretch out the heavens
And tread on the waves of the sea.
The universe springs from your word.
The stars themselves,
a moment's work.
In your timeless presence,
Silence is my only response.

What can I possibly say to you,
God of the ages?
You perform wonders
that cannot be fathomed,
Miracles that cannot be counted.

And yet you are so gentle,
eager to listen.
May I speak with courage
and with great humility.
I call out to you now.
It's all I can do.

Help me, Lord.
Keep me from failing you,
From failing to love you
And those you have called me to love.

Guide me, Holy Spirit.
Keep me in prayer.
I am so used to running,
So good at hiding.
Hold me close, Father;
Help me to do what is right
Even when I resist,
Even when every part of me
wants what is wrong,
Wants anything but your holy will.

Have pity on me, Lord Jesus.
You know the power of temptation,
The world and all its evil ways.
Give me strength against it;
Help me to carry my cross.

Teach me your ways, O Lord.
Hold me to your heart,
That I may come to truly know you,
Know that you are love itself,
And that your love endures forever,
Miraculously, even for me.

Amen.

TWELFTH DAY
EVENING

In 17th century Paris, a kitchen monk called Brother Lawrence wrote a simple book about what he deemed the most important of daily rituals: to practice the presence of God. Brother Lawrence claimed he felt as close to God while washing the dishes as he did while kneeling in the chapel because he was constantly practicing his awareness that God was always there. This prayer is written in that same vein—a mother walks through a routine day of service in the life of her family, accompanied by the very present reality of her Creator.

The evening prayer is written by Sandi, who grew up in Charlotte, North Carolina, and started attending Redeemer in 2000 after she married her husband, Bill. She was on staff with Redeemer Counseling Services for eight years before taking a break to stay home with her three young daughters. Now, Sandi serves in Redeemer's elementary after-school program, Kids Community Groups; teaches Sunday School classes and seminars; and coaches a Moms' Group at Redeemer.

"I pray regularly for wisdom in raising and discipling our daughters and for my further work in formal and lay counseling at Redeemer. The first prayer I ever remember praying was when I was seven years old that God would protect my mind from nightmares."

He called a little child to him...And he said: Truly I tell you, unless you change and become like little children, you will never enter the kingdom of heaven... Whoever welcomes one such child in my name welcomes me.

MATTHEW 18:2–5

HEAVENLY FATHER, I praise you this day because you are the perfect Parent. You love me fully and without condition. You are strong and mighty, yet generous and gracious in all your ways towards me. Thank you for calling me out of the darkness and into your glorious light. I am your beloved child now... loved, forgiven, saved, and made whole. You have saved me from myself. In your kindness and loving discipline, you are teaching me what it means to come to you as a little child.

You promise to provide everything I need for my various callings, as a professional, a laborer, or a parent. Even in my failings, you work all things together for good in our home. From dawn until dusk, you remind me of your love, provision, and faithfulness.

When I rise and face my inadequacy for the day ahead, you whisper into the depth of my heart that your grace is sufficient and your power is made perfect in my weakness. As I make breakfast, you remind me that you are the bread of life for our family. Your Word and your Spirit are our nourishment. As I run errands and do laundry, you remind me that you did not come to be served but to serve and to give your life as a ransom for many. Every act of mundane faithfulness matters to you.

I lose patience, but you are a God of perfect patience. As we fail each other, you show us the way to confess...and to forgive. When we snuggle in at bedtime, I am reminded that you are the God of all comfort. We are known. We are loved. As we review our days, we pray and give thanks for all that you have done for us and ask that we would be comforted by the reality that you will take the brokenness of our days, of our lives, and bring hope and restoration as you work all things for our good and for your glory.

As the children pray, they ask you for anything and everything, believing without doubt that you hear them and will answer them. Teach me what it means to walk by such faith and not by sight. Help me to trust you, Daddy. As the children grow, may they love those around them from the deep reservoir of love you have poured out into their hearts. Use them, in whatever arenas you call them, to be salt and light in this city you love.

THIRTEENTH DAY
MORNING

This writer praises God for the simple goodness of a cup of coffee and the complex beauty of "Appalachian Spring." With gentle humor, he pauses to reflect that God's goodness is evident all around us. He exemplifies how we might pray in an attitude of sincere appreciation for all the wonders of this life.

≋

The morning prayer is written by Dan, who was born and raised in the West. A New Yorker for 10 years, he has been at Redeemer since 2005. In his words, "Former pursuits include: actor, waiter, theatrical producer, law student, private equity lawyer. Current pursuits: entertainment lawyer, husband, and newish dad to a two-and-a-half-year-old. Future pursuits: opening a quiet bar on the Upper West Side and becoming a professional walker."

"My first prayer at age eight: 'Dear Maker of Heaven and Earth, please keep the rain away so that I can play baseball today.'"

The heavens declare the glory of God;
the skies proclaim the work of his hands.

PSALM 19:1

THE HEAVENS DECLARE your glory, and the sky proclaims your work. Each day pours out your speech, and each night reveals your knowledge.

Yet there are no words, and so I forget. I'm distracted. More than that, I'm driven. I want comfort, I want to scratch the itch, I want the good word from him or her or them.

But then your good word reveals itself. You made me. Not just that, you made me like you. And though I fell, you scooped me up and put me on your shoulders. The good things I have today can never be taken, the bad things will be worked together for good, and the best is ahead. That's not sentiment, but solid and valuable as gold. Sweeter than honey. Righteous and true altogether.

Let me consider the following: Coffee. The last four minutes of "Appalachian Spring." My daughter's fascination with socks. The miracle of email. An unnecessary dispute avoided, an important fight had, an unexpected solution. The subway train pulling into the station just as I arrive on the platform. Or the subway train pulling out of the station just as I arrive on the platform. Something rather than nothing. All gifts. All from you.

Now let me consider Jesus Christ. Lord Jesus, you created all these things. They were created for you. Yet you gave them up for me. You became estranged from them, from the Father, for me. For us. You've made my story, our story, a comedy instead of a tragedy. It all ends with a wedding and a feast, not death and a bloody stage. You are worthy of praise.

Lord Jesus, today I live and move and exist in you. This is a mystery. Help me to recognize and praise you for good things, and to know you better through suffering and disappointment.

Holy Spirit, protect me from my presumption, and open my eyes to the glory of Father, Son, and Spirit. Reign in this world, my world, today. Make my words and thoughts acceptable to you, my Rock and my Redeemer.

Psalm 19

THIRTEENTH DAY
EVENING

"I wrote this upon finding out that my dad was diagnosed with cancer," says the writer of this prayer. "I needed to hear truth and hope in my conversations with God." It is in times like these that we desperately need what this writer calls a deep and steadfast hope. In Christ we have a hope that is more than simple positive thinking. It is grounded in the life of Jesus, whose death conquered death itself and gave us a promise of abundant and eternal life.

〜

The evening prayer is written by Melissa, a research scientist who works in a lab exploring the differences between healthy cells and cancer cells. As a military kid, she learned that home is where your family lives (hers is currently in Texas). Melissa has been in New York City and attending Redeemer since 2012.

"I grew up in the church with my Christian mother and Jewish father, but my mom died of brain cancer when I was 13. I walked away from the church a couple years later, but when I was 19, I found my mom's old Bible and saw she had written, 'There is no greater joy to me than to know my children walk with the Lord.' That was the first time I truly wanted to talk to God as who he is instead of who I wanted him to be. That's when my life changed."

And I heard a loud voice from the throne, saying,
"Behold, the tabernacle of God is among men, and He will dwell among them,
and they shall be His people, and God Himself will be among them,
He will wipe every tear from their eyes. There will be no more death, or mourning
or crying or pain, for the old order of things has passed away."
And He who sits on the throne said, "Behold, I am making all things new."

REVELATION 21:3–5A

FATHER, I KNOW you hear the cries of the brokenhearted. You care deeply about healing what is broken and making things new. If it were not so, you would not have allowed your son to be broken, so that we might be made whole. May those who are struggling with broken hearts be reminded of this truth, especially those who grieve the loss of a parent.

You let us see beautiful moments of healing and creation at times in our lives, and I hope for these gifts every day. But you've also already given us a true and steadfast hope. You gave us your son who loves you and us so much he was willing to die for us. His death and resurrection are a promise that neither evil nor suffering have the last word. Nor does death. Nor does cancer.

One day, all will be healed, and all will be made new. I often put my hope in a lesser narrative of self-advancement or survival, but, my God, you desire more. You desire more for your creation. You desire for us to thrive as your image-bearers and cultivate spaces for flourishing in every sphere of our lives.

You faithfully beckon us back to your story time and time again, inviting us to contribute a word. Help us act out our better roles as supporting characters in your great narrative instead of trying to write a story of our own. May we let your Spirit teach us again what it means to be a child who wholly trusts in the goodness of our Father.

In Jesus' name, Amen.

FOURTEENTH DAY
MORNING

This writer, a physician, knows that no breath of life is guaranteed to follow the previous one. Each is a gift, made possible by God the Creator and sustained by God the Great Physician. Her prayer reminds us that in all things God is sovereign—meaning, he can do what he wants—but he is also good, and he only chooses to act out of love.

◁≋▷

The morning prayer is written by Cortessa, an ICU doctor, anesthesiologist, wife, and mother to three children. A Texas transplant who lives on the Upper West Side, she has been attending Redeemer for 10 years.

"Extending hospitality to the orphan and the sojourner makes me feel God's glory. That hospitality usually involves food and cocktails. I have been blessed to have been born to a Christian family, and cut my teeth on church pews. Although it wasn't until medical school that he became real to me. And then he became everything.

My first prayer memory is also my first answered prayer. I was in fifth grade, and my parents were upset at an extra-credit assignment I hadn't completed (typical immigrants). I prayed they would realize this was extra credit, that I wasn't irresponsible (typical first-born). Later, they expressed understanding and love."

The Lord gives, and the Lord takes away, blessed be the name of the Lord.

JOB 1:21

FOR YOUR sovereignty that covers each beat of my heart, I praise you.

For your love that covers each stirring of my soul, I glorify you.

For your kindness that covers each thought of my mind, I worship you.

For your grace that covers each expenditure of my strength, I thank you.

I commit the work of my hands to you. All my work is because of you, is for you, is my act of worship to you. You equipped me with these skills and placed me here, so enable and strengthen me to do your good work. I ask for your favor and your blessing to cover my actions, help me make the right decisions, bring to my mind things I have overlooked. I ask you, by your Holy Spirit, the same Spirit that raised Jesus Christ from the dead, please anoint me to live and breathe Christ to everyone I find. And to those people, in humility, help me meet them where they are, emotionally and spiritually. Give me grace, compassion, and patience.

Lord, you are the Great Physician. You crafted our bodies, the greatest designs in all creation. And yet, because of the fall, they are broken. Our bodies betray us; they fail us. But you are Lord over it all. I bring our broken bodies to you and ask for your healing. You have said,

"By your stripes we are healed." Expand our view of healing to consider the total healing and reconciliation you achieved on the cross. Help us pray for healing, increase our faith to pray for it. Help us believe you for it.

So often, you don't heal physically, in the time and fashion that we desire. In these moments, lead us to cast our disappointment at your feet, remembering that if you are big enough to handle our requests for healing, you are big enough to handle our grief. In our sadness, remind us that you weep with us. You are tender, and have suffered everything we have. You remain the lifter of our heads, the one who will wipe away every tear. By your Holy Spirit, bring your word to us, give us the words to preach to ourselves, and remind us of the truth of who you are.

Lord, you have restored us into communion with you; you have made us co-heirs with Christ. And that is enough. You don't owe us anything. But you, in your infinite mercy and kindness to us, give us so much more. You came so that we might have not only life, but *abundant life*. For you are sovereign, and you will give beauty for ashes. What others intend for evil, you intend for good.

FOURTEENTH DAY
EVENING

It may feel odd to pray for financiers and hedge fund investors. But remember we are all God's children and bear his image. Beyond praying for these people, we ought to pray, as the prophets did, for systemic justice and fairness in the economic system—as this prayer, written by an economist, does so well.

The evening prayer is written by Douglas, who grew up in Memphis, Tennessee, in a pastor's family. He moved to New York in 2011 to work for an economic forecasting firm and started attending Redeemer immediately. While a proud southerner, Douglas says he may never return home because he loves New York City so much.

"My first true spiritual memory was at age 11 at a camp in northeast Alabama. I began to question: 'Why did Jesus have to die? Why couldn't God just wave his hand and forgive us without sacrifice?' After conversation and deeper understanding, I thanked God for his mercy and salvation."

Then the LORD spoke to Job out of the storm.

JOB 38:1

Y OU ARE LORD AND RULER over all things. You set limits for the clouds and dam the waters of the sea. You replenish storehouses of snow and sustain the sun's blaze. Likewise, you direct the paths of prime ministers, soldiers, and beggars. You are God over art and science.

What is more, you are ruler over the world, even the world of finance. You, Lord, understand economics better than the Nobel laureate; you grasp the complex financial instrument better than the Wall Street banker. Not only do you sustain all earthly life, you also sustain all earthly institutions because you are their ultimate author. I am grateful that nothing escapes your understanding or care—that I worship a God who is above both the Himalayas and the global financial system. I am in awe of your vastness and your infinite and eternal creativity.

Please forgive us for failing to properly engage your creation. Your Word instructs us to act thoughtfully and mercifully. Yet we are guilty of either retreating from the world or engaging in economic exploitation.

I pray that you would impart wisdom to us, your creatures. You are the God of truth; therefore, let us drink deeply of truth. Supply bright and bold minds to plumb the depths of economic theory—that they might return with richer intuition and knowledge. And grant policymakers the courage to enact prudent policy that enables all members of society to flourish. Moreover, encourage us, your body, to engage in politics and commerce with greater awareness.

Likewise, remove our sinful tendency toward unfair gain. Grant us zeal for justice and a heart for the poor. I pray that we would pursue the welfare of the marginalized with the same fervor that we pursue professional excellence. For all who work as bankers and traders and investors, God, make their love of knowledge greater than their love of money and make their love of people greater than their love of knowledge. Make them responsible stewards of the great influence they wield.

Finally, I pray for a strong economy to provide jobs and dignity for all.

In Jesus' name, Amen.

FIFTEENTH DAY
MORNING

New York is a hard-charging city. In the city that never sleeps, the people are never still. They are logging countless hours on the literal and figurative running paths of the city. This is not only true of New York, of course. All of us are working more and resting less; we are the always-on generation. This writer, a runner herself, leads us to slow down and ask: "What are we running for? And what are we running from? Might we rise today and, to paraphrase the English runner Eric Liddell, run simply because we feel God's pleasure?"

The morning prayer is written by Elizabeth, who is from Ann Arbor, Michigan, and moved to New York for a job in finance. She now works part-time as a fundraising strategist and consultant, serving small and start-up nonprofits and spending the balance of her week as a mom to two little girls. She and her husband are both runners. Elizabeth began attending Redeemer sporadically starting in 2001 and full time in 2006. She currently serves on the Diaconate and in the Meals Ministry.

"As a very young girl, I prayed, 'Lord, please watch over my family as we sleep tonight.'"

Therefore, since we are surrounded by such a great cloud of witnesses,
let us throw off everything that hinders and the sin that so easily entangles.
And let us run with perseverance the race marked out for us...

HEBREWS 12:1

HEAVENLY FATHER, HOLY GOD, I come before you as an empty, restless sinner saved by grace.

I am anxious, consumed by an ache that seeps into the deepest corners of my mind. If you, oh Lord, kept a record of sins, surely I would not stand.

I run and run until I can no longer breathe, struggling to reach some unknown and unattainable finish line— and yet this ache, this longing, this desire for something I cannot articulate follows me wherever I go.

With Satan prowling like a lion, ready to pounce, I am thinking "I, I, I" when true life is found in thinking "You, You, You."

Forgive me, Lord, and reorient my heart towards your brilliance, glory, and the deep, quenching rest you offer.

Sweet, fierce Jesus, open my heart to your pursuit and chase away this restlessness. If you so care for the lilies of the field, surely you will provide for my every need, in ways known and unknown, seen and unseen.

Our city is full of runners—those who log mile after mile, both literally and figuratively. May our primary and ultimate finish line be a life overflowing with praise for you, the one true provider of freedom, forgiveness, and grace.

In you, I find deep and lasting rest.

Suddenly, I see you everywhere, anew. In the tender sigh of the newborn, you are here. In the laughter, in the sand, in the warm bed, in the written word, in the outstretched hand—you are here, and there, and here again—and you have provided me with unimaginable abundance, beginning and ending on the cross.

Draw me to you more each day, and with every breath, Lord. You are my starting place and my finish line, and in you I am found, complete and whole. I fix my eyes on you, Jesus, and drink deeply from your well to run with perseverance the race you've marked out for me, in this city and well beyond.

Amen.

FIFTEENTH DAY
EVENING

The fall has broken us in myriad ways, but we have hope of healing. The path to our sanctification is long and often painful. Someone in a bad physical accident cannot relearn how to walk without extensive therapy and training. One cannot learn to walk the path of Christ without similar effort, time, and assistance. The writer of this prayer reminds himself of the comforting truth that each step might be ordered and guided by a God who is both unfathomably powerful and mercifully tender.

The evening prayer is written by Jonathan, who was a missionary kid, born and raised in Costa Rica. He has lived in Boston, New Jersey, Pennsylvania, Miami, and Chicago. He moved to New York, attended Columbia University for graduate school, and fell in love with his wife and this city. He now makes his living as a physical therapist. He says he professed belief in God as a child but "kicked and screamed against the church" until attending college, where he says he met Christ, truly, for the first time.

"I first prayed in Costa Rica, in a small mountainside church where services were frequented by wandering chickens. At five years old, I prayed to God under the attention of a lion hand-puppet worked by a charismatic Spanish-speaking female ventriloquist. I still recall feeling that the lion's mouth felt suspiciously like a human hand."

For physical training is of some value, but godliness has value for all things,
holding promise for both the present life and the life to come.

1 TIMOTHY 4:8

FATHER... We are constantly searching to fulfill our own desires. The impossibility of getting everything we want drives us to look for help. And the help we seek, oh God, to our great privilege, comes from you. Cover your world, your city, and your church with your sustaining hand and hear our prayers.

You are the one whose fingers nimbly arrange order out of expanding chaos. You are the one whose song the morning stars linger to sing. You are the one whose very words bring light out of darkness and life out of death. At the end of the day, I bend before you and ask that you would set my heart to tick in time with yours, that my desires might be your desires.

My hope rests in you, who limped under the splinters of a wooden cross so that we might be freed. Jesus, you were exposed and scarred so that we might be saved. Were the very sun extinguished from the horizon, still you would not abandon us. That day on the cross, the sun was covered and the ground shook, but you did not abandon your beloved.

You were crushed, the promised cornerstone, under the weight of dusty death. But you crushed death itself.

It is with that knowledge that I pray tonight. I come before you confessing the sins of my day. Help me to remember that you took death so that I might have life. Tomorrow may I not repeat the sins of today but instead live more fully for you.

Be thou my vision, oh Lord of my heart, naught be all else to me save that thou art, thou my best thought, by day or by night, waking or sleeping, thy presence my light.

Holy Spirit, sweep through us that our hearts might be tilled,

That with your whispered teachings our souls might be filled.

May I learn how to walk more closely with you by leaning on your everlasting arms. And may the words of my mouth and the meditation of my heart be pleasing to you, oh God!

Amen.

Be Thou My Vision. Irish Hymn. (CA. 700)

SIXTEENTH DAY
MORNING

Do you really understand those who are suffering, or do you just think you do? Do you see who is left behind when the rest of society is flourishing, or do you assume "everyone must be doing alright?" This writer asks God for deeper empathy, deeper understanding, and a deeper love for the city.

The morning prayer is written by Glen, who, with his wife Carole, is an original founder of Redeemer. Glen continues to serve as an elder in the church, while also directing a ministry for the poor called Here's Life Inner City, whose mission is to connect, empower, and develop local churches that are sensitive to the needs of the poor and marginalized.

For the entire law is fulfilled in keeping this one command:
"Love your neighbor as yourself."

GALATIANS 5:14

THANK YOU, LORD, for impressing me with the truth and power of the gospel. You have changed me.

You have been faithful to me now for years. Help me to not take you for granted. Oh Lord, help me appreciate your continual working in my life, my family's life, and in my world.

Help me to be excited about trusting you, more than ever, as society makes seismic shifts. Let me see these cultural changes as opportunities to apply the gospel in new ways in my life and world.

In a polarized nation, I know how hard it is to practice true empathy and put myself in the shoes of someone else. Help me see others as you see them, especially those who feel marginalized. Even when I don't understand their viewpoint or don't agree with it, help me to "take on their burden," as stated in Galatians 5. I want to relate to people with compassion, even risking the awkwardness of misunderstanding.

In my time, I have seen how you can change a neighborhood and how an entire city can change. I praise you for lower rates of crime, rising rates of employment, and the increased popularity of urban living. However, I also recognize that even good things come at a cost. Let me not lose sight of the "collateral damage" on those who are struggling to afford their housing and those who have been displaced. Let me not lose sight of those who aren't participating in the progress enjoyed by most. And let them not be forgotten by our leaders in the city and in our churches. Oh Lord, show us how to trust you with the effects of our prayers for the city to become a good place to live, even as that now affects some citizens in negative ways.

As you demonstrate compassion on your children, help me to show compassion to my neighbor—daily, consistently, joyfully. I ask this in the name of Jesus. Amen.

SIXTEENTH DAY
EVENING

Like the author of the morning prayer, this writer asks that the eyes of our heart may be opened so that we might see the need around us and respond. It is so much easier to assume we are not so blind. It is much harder to cultivate a healthy skepticism of our hearts' abilities to see. We are broken in a thousand different ways and are most blind to our own blindness. We need God to remove the scales from our eyes.

The evening prayer is written by Eirini, who grew up in Cairo, Egypt, and moved to New Jersey with her family when she was a teen. A manager at a global manufacturing company, she has been attending Redeemer for 12 years, and hosts a Community Group at her apartment.

"I always went to church, but I fell in love with Jesus when I was 23. I am amazed at who he is and the lengths he went to for a friendship with me. I don't remember my first prayer. But I remember my first desperate prayer. I made a mistake at work and all my striving to prove myself as 'having it together' crumbled before my eyes. I realized that moment that if it were not for God's grace, I would have/be nothing!"

I pray that the eyes of your heart may be enlightened
in order that you may know the hope to which he has called you,
the riches of his glorious inheritance in his holy people...

EPHESIANS 1:18

OUR GRACIOUS FATHER and king, I come before you today full of thanksgiving for who you are. You are glorious for the amazing work of creation, for your saving love for me, for welcoming me into your presence, and for including me in your plan to restore our world. Because you know my frame, I come to put my prayers before you.

In your love, remember those of us who are lonely. Show your guiding hand that we may be assured of your abiding presence. Make us a community that notices, welcomes, and encourages the forgotten. In this very transient city, I ask you to give us life-giving friendships that assure us we belong to each other and to you. I hang on Jesus' prayer that you would make us one.

In your grace, remember those in need of resources—physical, emotional, and spiritual. The uncertainties around us confront us with how inadequate we are in securing our future. We have no hope but for your kindness; we have no peace but for the kind you give; we have no hiding place but for the one you provide. Shepherd us through the uncertainties until we place our trust in you. Open our eyes and let us discover you faithful to the very end and loving beyond our wildest dreams. I hang onto your words that you will never leave us and that you will indeed wipe away every tear, from Egypt to East Harlem.

For your glory, let me know the magnitude of your love and sacrifice for us. Only that would show us how valuable we are to you; only that can transform us into agents of your love in the world, who bring good news to the poor and to everyone nearby. Let my heart be excited and expectant for what you are doing in my midst, in my day. I hang on your love.

Give ear, O God, and hear; open your eyes and see our city and the people who bear your Name. We do not make requests of you because we are righteous, but because of your great mercy.

In the name of your son, Jesus,

Amen.

SEVENTEENTH DAY
MORNING

This writer reminds us that our calling is not to own resources but to steward resources that belong to God. Jesus warned people repeatedly to be on guard against allowing a love of money to dominate their lives. Money breeds an anti-God belief in human self-sufficiency, as if it could be the rock, the foundation, of our lives. This prayer is an opportunity to re-order our loves properly.

The morning prayer is written by Dan, a wealth advisor and financial planner who is also an elder at Redeemer. Originally from St. Louis, Dan moved to New York City and found Redeemer in 1994. He is married and lives with his wife and sons on the Upper West Side.

"I was 27 when I first came to believe. My first prayer was 'Lord, save me.'"

The earth is the LORD's, and everything in it, the world, and all who live in it.

PSALM 24:1

For you know the grace of our Lord Jesus Christ, that though he was rich, yet for your sake he became poor, so that you through his poverty might become rich.

2 CORINTHIANS 8:9

Do not store up for yourselves treasures on earth, where moths and vermin destroy, and where thieves break in and steal. But store up for yourselves treasures in heaven, where moths and vermin do not destroy, and where thieves do not break in and steal. For where your treasure is, there your heart will be also.

MATTHEW 6:19–21

L ORD,
Everything good in all of creation comes from you. Everything that I have comes from you. I am just a steward of my possessions. I brought nothing into this world and will take nothing with me when I leave. It is only right to acknowledge you as the true and rightful owner.

Forgive me for taking credit for my accomplishments, for taking ownership of my possessions, and for not giving thanks for all of your gifts. Forgive me for being envious towards those who have more than I do, for being prideful towards those who have less than I do, and for pining after too many comforts in this life. I know that the measure of a man is not found in his net worth, but I often act as if the opposite were true. Too often, in seeking financial security, I am less than compassionate towards the poor. Lord, through your grace, you gave away your greatest treasure in Jesus Christ, your only son, for our sake.

Lord, let your immeasurable sacrifice for me make me a more generous person, a more faithful and thankful person. I know that generosity is not so much about how much I give, but how I live. To be a good steward is not simply giving a tithe or living below my means. It means I need to give up ownership of everything I have and make seeing Jesus in heaven my real treasure. Let me give careful thought to how I spend, save, and give away what you have entrusted to me. I pray that your kingdom will come on earth as it is in heaven, where our treasure is not measured in what we have, but in whom we place our trust.

In Jesus' name, Amen.

SEVENTEENTH DAY
EVENING

This writer begins by addressing God by some of the various names he takes in Scripture. Saying the names and reflecting on them calls to mind some of God's different attributes. And in this prayer they most clearly call out God's nature as "Father."

≈

The evening prayer is written by Amanda, who hails from Louisville, Kentucky, and moved to New York City in 2010. She volunteers with the Kids Community Group, Vacation Bible School, preschool missions month, and as a member of the prayer team.

"In first grade, I prayed to God that if my teacher called on me to be first in line that I would really know he existed. She called on me first. It felt like such a miracle! I don't think I heard the gospel and experienced the need for a Savior until I was 21 years old, through the help of a staff member of CRU college ministry."

*Therefore confess your sins to each other
and pray for each other so that you may be healed.*

JAMES 5:16A

DEAR Lord, *Abba* Father, Jehovah-jireh (the Lord who provides), Prince of Peace, Father of mercies and compassion, Elohim (the all-knowing, all-powerful Creator of the Universe), the one who binds the broken heart, the great I AM.

I lift up the children in our church and across this city. I ask:

That our children would walk in your truth, as it brings you no greater joy than to hear your children walk in the truth.

That they would call you *Abba* Father, know you as their father, and have a personal relationship with you.

That they would believe your promises to steadfastly love them, forgive them always, be slow to anger, all powerful, sovereign and in control of a future that is for their good and your glory.

That this generation of children would grow and remain in your vine, marry strong Christian counterparts, love you in word and deed, and know you forever, rejoicing and thanking you as you raise up the next generation after that.

I pray for the volunteers and teachers who work with our children. Help them know and feel with all their hearts your love for them. Lord, I also ask for your Holy Spirit to strengthen parents who are trying to humbly lead their children. May they act in line with the Spirit of truth.

Lord, teach the children and volunteers to love you with all their hearts, souls, and minds. And to love their neighbors as themselves. This is what you want from us. Teach us to abide in Christ and be made into a new creation where we can glorify you in all we do. We need you, Lord. Please let us be in your presence, experience you, and overflow with gratitude.

Lord, keep our children safe. May they come and go without harm. Keep them in good health. Preserve and protect each one.

Finally Lord, may I remember I, too, am a child, your child. May my faith be not childish, but childlike—pure, confident, and thankful.

Amen.

3 John 1:4, Romans 8:28, John 15:5, Matthew 22:37

EIGHTEENTH DAY
MORNING

Many people imagine God as one in Greek legend: with a stern face, long beard, and thunderbolts to hurl. Yet the tenderness of God is evident in both the New Testament and Old. We apparently give him joy. This writer knows that God "rejoices over us with singing," and she asks for reminders of his ever-present love. And if he so rejoices over us, then we can confidently come to him with requests that he would guide us and provide for us. And we, like this writer, can pray not only for ourselves but for the many people sharing the streets of our city.

The morning prayer is written by Lori, a playwright, screenwriter, and teacher. Originally from East Moline, Illinois, she started attending Redeemer in 1999. She regularly reads Scripture at worship services, serves on the prayer team, and has co-led Community Groups.

"The first time I prayed, I was around six years old. In a tiny church in East Moline, Illinois, a woman told me the story of Jesus and then asked me if I'd like to pray. I'll never forget that moment, when I believed God was listening and could hear me."

The LORD your God is with you, the Mighty Warrior who saves.
He will take great delight in you; in his love he will no longer rebuke you,
but will rejoice over you with singing."

ZEPHANIAH 3:17

FATHER, GOD, Holy Friend, Maker of the mountains and the mandarinfish! In your kindness, you color each blade of grass and each splendid leaf. You are worthy of praise, and I thank you for your faithfulness towards us. With delight and tender care, you sing over me.

Lord, I ask that you would guide me today and throughout this coming week. I long to be chosen—by my bosses, friends, family, and powers that be. Help me believe that in you I am already chosen, loved. Cause me to recall who I belong to. Holy Spirit, right now, this week, and throughout this year, remind me that I am a son of the Most High King and an heir to your kingdom.

Be regularly on my mind, Lord. Replace my busy brain with thoughts of the resurrection. You have made me cell by cell. You have my very hairs numbered. Oh, how you love me, Father. You are the Maker of the Universe, and yet you care about my details. Saturate me, Jesus, with the knowledge of your great love. Quench my thirsty soul with your living water, Lord. Remind me again and again that you have conquered death and that you are ever-present with me.

For the actors in this city, looking for work and for validation; for the writers composing stories to make sense of life; for the producers looking to make a name for themselves: May they see that success or failure is fleeting but that you rejoice over us with singing.

For those who are struggling financially, would you send unexpected financial blessing? For those who are looking for work, would you open new doors? For those who feel forgotten, oppressed, overlooked, for those who wonder if you actually hear their prayers, Lord, would you be real to us, speak to us, and heal us?

I lift up the victims of violent crimes both here and around the world. Guard their broken hearts from bitterness. Would you surround them with signs of your grace? Would you help them to believe that your plan is good, even when their pain is overwhelming?

Heal me, Lord. Give me a humble courage and a healing presence. Cover me under the shadow of your wings. I ask in the name of my Lord and Savior Jesus Christ. Amen.

EIGHTEENTH DAY
EVENING

This writer prays about putting down roots where you are. She speaks of desiring to deepen connections with her neighbors so that she and her family might serve them more effectively. You get the feeling that this is someone who has internalized just how good God is and wants to live a life fueled by thankfulness.

❧

The evening prayer is written by Carrie, a wife and mother of three who serves as Redeemer's East Side Play & Learn coordinator and who volunteers with the nonprofit A House on Beekman. Her family has been in New York since 2012 and has attended the East Side morning service at Redeemer since their first Sunday here.

"My kids see New York City as their home. As a family, we have committed to this place. God encourages me with his creation story. While he did make the sky, water, etc., it is *people* who are the crown of his creation. With that in mind, I make roots in Manhattan.

I remember being so scared as a child during our pastor's sermon about hell and crying during the last hymn. My siblings went to Sunday School while Mom held me and Dad talked to me. Right there I prayed for Jesus to come into my heart and make me new. I was five."

Do nothing out of selfish ambition or vain conceit.
Rather, in humility value others above yourselves, not looking to your
own interests but each of you to the interests of the others.

PHILIPPIANS 2:3–4

MY FATHER, I am thankful as I come humbly and confidently to your feet. I know that it is Jesus' work on my behalf that earns this place in your presence. I come fully aware of my sin and overwhelmed by your mercy. You are holy, and your love for me is perfect.

Your purposes in me are a blessing. The fact that you have plans for my life is enough reason to be glad! Grant me the strength to follow you in daily obedience. I want to joyfully submit to your wisdom. Replace my fear with courage.

Fill me with your love. I want it to overflow to the people you have brought into my life. May the children in my family and all children of our congregation experience the love of Jesus. May they taste and see that you are good. Lord, make yourself known to them, even now, and be their refuge. Help them come to love your Word. Give them an appetite for it today so that they would grow to delight in your ways. I pray they will know the truth and power of your gospel, feeling its undeniable presence deep in their hearts and seeing its work throughout our city.

May I be "a vessel for honorable use, set apart as holy, useful to the master of the house, ready for every good work." May I be a part of the work you are doing to build your kingdom in this city. From soccer games to school socials, Father, I pray that my family and the families of our church would give evidence of how people can be changed by the gospel. God, deepen our roots and our friendships in this city to bring glory to your name. Bring into our home more friends who want to find out who you are. For your gospel is true. Redemption is real. The cross happened. Forbid it that I would live focused on anything else.

Make me responsive to your voice. Guide me. May I not delay, but inspire in me an urgency to serve. In your mercy, continue to open my eyes to opportunities to love my neighbors. Give us grace. Thank you for giving me everything I need in Jesus. I love you, Lord. May I daily grow better at showing this love in my life.

Amen.

2 Timothy 2:21

NINETEENTH DAY
MORNING

This writer fills her prayer with scriptural references. The picture of Jesus in the gospels shows that he was constantly quoting Scripture. Knowing the Scriptures and having them on the tip of your tongue is a wonderful resource for praying with the right perspective.

⁓

The morning prayer is written by Connie, a caregiver and receptionist. Connie and her husband, Joe, have lived in New York City for 28 years and are raising four kids in the city.

"I moved from Union Springs, New York, to New York City with my husband and a five-year plan: pursue our acting careers, experience all of New York, and then move someplace 'safe and normal' to start a family. Then we heard a sermon on Jeremiah and the City at Redeemer and committed to God to stay in the city and raise our family here instead. My first prayer was the Lord's Prayer."

God is our refuge and strength, an ever-present help in trouble.
Therefore we will not fear, though the earth give way and the mountains
fall into the heart of the sea...

PSALM 46:1-2

FATHER, SON, HOLY SPIRIT, Thank you for being our God of inconceivable strength and power, of approachable counsel and guidance, and of intimate love who dwells within us.

You brought forth wisdom
  as the first of your works,
You appointed wisdom
  from eternity, before the world began.

Please impart your wisdom on the leaders of our world, our country, our city, and our families.

LORD, I acknowledge before you the violence, destruction, and dysfunction that surrounds us on a daily basis. At times, it makes it hard to catch our breath. At your heart is a compassionate concern for the broken and desperate.

Your Word says that you are our refuge and our fortress, our God in whom we trust. Your faithfulness will be our shield and rampart. Please stretch out your healing hand across our world, our country, our city, our families, and our hearts.

LORD, overwhelm us with who you are that our sadness may be uplifted. Remind us that the world is a veneer of vanity and contains nothing that can bring our souls lasting contentment. Revive our dying spirits, and restore or make new our passionate devotion to you. Deepen our humility, and lessen our fears that we may have the courage to admit our pride to ourselves, to each other, and to you. Grant us the gift of humor that assists to endure the unbearable. Change our hearts to seek another's needs over our own.

For we know that if you change our hearts, you will change our families, our city, our country, and our world. Teach us to "be joyful always, pray continually, and be thankful in all circumstances."

In Jesus Christ's name, we pray. Amen.

Psalm 107, Psalm 91, 1 Thessalonians 5

NINETEENTH DAY
EVENING

As you read the scriptures you notice how God, again and again, disturbs the comfortable and comforts the disturbed. The great danger of material comfort is, by never knowing hunger or thirst or great need, we fail to feel the need for a Provider or a Savior. Our full cupboards and full bellies deceive us into thinking that our lives are full. But our hearts tell us otherwise. We need the filling of the Holy Spirit. And we need to realize that it is in emptying ourselves on behalf of others that our lives feel most full.

※

The evening prayer is written by John and Summer, who are married with four children and live on the Upper East Side. John was born and raised in Montgomery, Alabama, Summer in Baton Rouge, Louisiana. They came to New York in the fall of 2005 for John's job and started attending Redeemer in spring of 2006. John has served as an elder for three years, and Summer leads a Women's Community Group on Tuesday mornings. They also host a Community Group in their home on Tuesday nights. John works at a small investment firm; Summer is at home with their four children.

"We both were brought up in the Episcopal Church, and so we memorized the Lord's Prayer as young children."

Come, all you who are thirsty, come to the waters; and you who have no money, come, buy and eat!...Why spend money on what is not bread, and your labor on what does not satisfy?

ISAIAH 55:1–2

YOUR WORD SAYS, "Come everyone who thirsts, come to the waters."

What if I am not thirsty? I don't know if I have ever truly felt a thirst that was unmet.

Your Word says, "He who has no money, come, buy and eat!" What if I am not hungry? What if I do have money and can buy things, even things beyond my basic needs?

Your Word says, "Why do you labor for that which does not satisfy?" Why is it, at the end of the day, when the world tells me all is well and that I should be satisfied, why is it that I get a feeling that there is something missing? Something is unfilled. I am blessed. I am not hungry, and I am not thirsty. And yet, still, I am not satisfied.

Jesus, you said you are the living water, and that the "waters" I can obtain through my own works will never quench the deep thirst of my soul. Even though I have known this for years, decades even, I continue to find myself lost in my own efforts. My labors have brought myriad comforts and yet made me ignore that which will satisfy my deeper needs.

When I rest in my own strength and start to think that I am no longer thirsty or hungry, I know I am lost. When I get the sense that I can take care of everything I need, Lord, please, show me my brokenness. Show me my need. Show me that the only reason my labors accomplish anything at all is by your grace and your provision. When the comforts of my life threaten to drown out the still, small voice that tells me of my need for you, let me feel my spiritual drought acutely. When my cupboards and closet and checking account are full, remind me that without Jesus, I am spiritually empty. Bring me again and again to the place where, despite the world's riches, I am thirsty, hungry, dying to myself—so that I may seek and find you, and in you only be satisfied.

And God forbid it that I should focus only on myself when there are in this city those who thirst, both physically and spiritually, those who have no currency, those who through addiction or mental illness are homeless and alone. Provide for them. Bless the shelters with food and money and workers. And make me ever more generous in stewarding your resources toward them.

TWENTIETH DAY
MORNING

Sometimes, the most powerful prayers are the ones in which we remember all that God has promised.

❧

The morning prayer is written by Ben, who hails from Rhode Island, moved to New York in 1997, and began attending Redeemer in 2001. He has served as a Community Group leader and an elder. He works at an executive recruiting firm, helping individuals find work that matches their abilities and calling.

"I pray for the wisdom to remind myself that I am dependent on God, not on my own skills and abilities. I pray for the people I interact with and for the ability and mindset to do my work unto the Lord, not just unto my clients and my own performance. My first prayer was Psalm 23: 'The Lord is my Shepherd, I shall not want.'"

You did not choose me, but I chose you and appointed you
so that you might go and bear fruit—fruit that will last—and so that
whatever you ask in my name the Father will give you.

JOHN 15:16

O GOD, "I AM," the Eternal and Everlasting God, you chose me, and you promise to have your Holy Spirit continually guide me. I know that your aim is not to guide me in the path of comfort or pleasure or a nice lifestyle or admiration of people. Your aim is to guide me in the path of righteousness. You do this for your Name's sake and not for my own glory. I truly don't want to do life without you, even though I often forget.

You are my Lord and not my landlord. More than that, you are my Father, and you want to treat me as your child. Help me to act like the prodigal younger son. I know you will always be willing, like that father, to take me back, but help me to not wander away from you in the first place. I want to seek you with all my heart. I want to better understand you because I know that your ways are not my ways and your thoughts are not my thoughts.

O to grace, how great a debtor daily I'm constrained to be! Let thy goodness, like a fetter, bind my wandering heart to thee. I'm prone to wander. Lord, I feel it. I'm prone to leave the God I love. Here's my heart, O take and seal it, seal it for thy courts above.

I believe; help my unbelief! It is vain for me to rise up early and go to work without seeking you first. I know you want to give to those you love, even in their sleep. Yet I want to do it myself. Or I want to, but I do not think I have the time, or other things make it difficult to do. I do not make this time with you the priority it needs to be. It is not the example that Jesus showed me. By not being in daily community with you, I do not let you do what you want to do in and through my life. I give up so much of what you would and could do in me, and I diminish your work through me in others.

I confess this time of seeking you is not just preparation for the real work of my day; it *is* the work, and it needs to be the most important thing. I want to live life with joy and gratitude, mindful of what you have done. Let my heart and my calendar prepare you room.

O Lord, please bless me and tune my heart to sing thy praise. I join with heaven and nature and the saints to praise the Lord. Amen.

Come Thou Fount of Every Blessing. Robinson, Robert. (1757)

TWENTIETH DAY
EVENING

If we are honest, one of the most penetrating questions we can ask ourselves is whether we want God or we want the gifts God provides. Do we want a relationship with our Creator, or do we just want him to make our lives easy? A good way to uncover the real answer to this question is to look at how much time we spend in prayer asking for things we want and how much time we spend thanking God for what we have and seeking how we might give him glory by using what we have for others. This writer devotes his prayer to the latter, clearly using his evening reflection to seek a stronger relationship with God.

The evening prayer is written by Samuel, a grant-maker. He traded life in sunny Southern California for the rough and tumble of New York City five years ago and serves on Redeemer's Downtown prayer team.

"Redeemer has been an anchor for my faith ever since I arrived. One of my earliest prayers was for a little brother. I was no more than five at the time, and I told my parents I wanted a brother. They encouraged me to pray, and so I did."

As for the rich in this present age, charge them not to be haughty,
nor to set their hopes on the uncertainty of riches, but on God, who richly provides
us with everything to enjoy. They are to do good, to be rich in good works,
to be generous and ready to share, thus storing treasure for themselves as a good
foundation for the future, so that they may take hold of that which is truly life.

I TIMOTHY 6:17-19

O LORD,
How richly you bless me with abundance, though I remember it not. You give me health, freedom and opportunity, family and friends—and yet I neglect to give thanks. You provide me with everything to enjoy, but I place my hope elsewhere.

Too often I make what is good into an idol. You give wealth, but I hoard it instead of sharing. The opportunities you give me become a source of pride, not a reason for gratitude. Friendship becomes a way to use others, not a way to bless them. Why? Why do I glory in things that I don't deserve? They won't even last. Moths and thieves and rust will make them disappear.

Father, teach me to glorify you with what you have given me. Open my eyes to the gifts you have bestowed. Show me how to bless others the way you blessed me. I count those blessings now: money for necessities, daily bread, shelter against storms, strength to walk, time for friends.

Help me to give joyfully with my time, my energy, and my money. Direct my steps to the greatest needs in the church, the city, and the world. You have placed me here among my neighbors. Help me to love them and serve them. You have placed me in this city; help me seek its welfare. You have placed me in this world; help me to show others your Kingdom here.

May I set my hope on you, my Rock, my Redeemer, my Provider. May I be rich in good works, not as a way to seek favor but as a way to give thanks. May I be generous and ready to share, knowing well how richly you have shared with me. How glorious it then will be!

I pray this in the name of your Son, who gave everything.

Amen.

TWENTY-FIRST DAY
MORNING

This dancer's prayer reminds us that in life we may constantly feel judged and like we must win the approval of the crowd, but that Christ has taken the ultimate judgment for us. He took on our poor performance as if it were his, suffering jeers and snickering, but even more—the lash and the nails. Because of that, we need not tiptoe through life, afraid of making mistakes. We may leap boldly, knowing that what mistakes we make will just prove again the robust and permanent grace of the gospel.

The morning prayer is written by Silas, who is originally from Charlotte, North Carolina. The youngest of seven children, he moved away from his family when he was 14 to complete his ballet training in New York at Lincoln Center's School of American Ballet. He has been dancing professionally with New York City Ballet for the past four years.

"I have attended Redeemer since I was 14. I became a believer while I was still a little boy, probably five or six. I remember having extended prayer times after our morning family devotions starting when I was very young, during which both parents and each of my six siblings and I had the opportunity to pray aloud. These are very special memories to me, hearing and participating in the habit of prayer."

*Wearing a linen ephod, David was dancing
before the LORD with all his might...*

2 SAMUEL 6:14

LORD JESUS, WHEN YOU ENTERED this world, you put on our human flesh. You experienced the limitations, pleasures, and pain of our embodied state. On the cross, you were crushed to make us whole. As your broken body was the instrument of our salvation, may our dancing bodies be the instruments of your praise as we take class, rehearse, and perform for you.

As I pursue excellence in my work, I know that total mastery is ultimately unattainable. But as I pursue holiness, may I be encouraged that my pursuit has you as its ultimately attainable goal.

As artists and performers find freedom in their art by first submitting to the constraints of technique, may I also find the joyful liberty that comes when I surrender my whole self to your Word and will.

As I constantly receive criticism and scrutiny from those in authority over me, and as I receive the private judgments from those who watch my every move, may I remember that yours is the final, and ultimately only, approval that matters.

I may put on a costume in preparation for the performance of the day, but forbid that I would put on a mask and hide who I am in you. May I be myself—vulnerable and honest—because in you I am my true self: confident and strong. May I remember that I am clothed in your righteousness and beauty.

Lord Jesus, you have masterfully choreographed all of history. As I play my part, give me the perseverance to dance each step well. And may the audience see in my performance not my skill but hints of your holiness and glimpses of your glory.

Amen.

TWENTY-FIRST DAY
EVENING

This writer takes the perspective of coming alongside someone in need and walking with them to help shoulder their burden. Who, in your life, could use your help and appreciate you coming alongside them, praying for them, helping them out? How might God use you to encourage someone around you today?

※

The evening prayer is written by Tim, who works in the residential recovery program at The Bowery Mission in New York City, helping men caught in the cycles of addiction, crime, and homelessness. He moved to New York City from Oklahoma with his wife, Suzy, and two daughters, Lindsey and Bethany, to "see what God was doing in the city." He admits that although the move from rural Oklahoma was incredibly stretching, they would do it again. Tim is a West Side elder. The family became members of Redeemer shortly after arriving.

"Though I was not raised in a church-attending family, my mother prayed nightly with me. My first nightly repeated prayer was the 'Now I lay me down to sleep; I pray the Lord my soul to keep,' prayer. I learned it by age four, and somehow it was significant to me."

You, LORD, hear the desire of the afflicted; you encourage them,
and you listen to their cry, defending the fatherless and the oppressed,
so that mere earthly mortals will never again strike terror.

PSALM 10:17–18

O LORD, TONIGHT there are many in this city who are afflicted with suffering, who are in tears and at the end of their rope. They are homeless or jobless. Some are friendless, too. I know you hear their prayers and you see their tears. Please strengthen them.

How will we ever make sense of the mess we call our lives? How do we live with what we have done—what we have seen? How do we put one foot in front of the other, Lord? Enable us to bear up, Lord. Help us carry this, Lord, for I have no answers to give. I've got nothing.

Except an ear.

I can listen. I can point to you, for your ears—they are inclined toward us. You hear our cries and feel our pain. You've been there, haven't you, Lord? You are no stranger to pain; you know rejection. You stood among the criminals; you've been convicted. You've been lonely.

You've been abandoned. You know all too well the pain of hunger. You know what it is to thirst. Your bones ached and your body bled. You know suffering and you know death.

But you overcame that, Lord. And you have used it for good. You and only you can bring something from all of this, something worthwhile, something worth waiting on. Remind me, Lord, that you see us and hear us, and know us. We are not alone, for you are here. You have sent the Comforter, your Holy Spirit, to help.

Lead us into our futures and out of our sorrows. Make sense of our troubles and our pain. Give us next steps. Give us hope. Lord, grow our faith. Help us to believe. Strengthen our hearts. According to your love for us, hold us up, for we need you.

Amen.

TWENTY-SECOND DAY
MORNING

This writer, a museum producer, contemplates how we may learn about God by studying his creation. What are we looking for when we pass through a museum or a gallery? Inspiration? Distraction? Truth? Do we even know what we want? Might we see, as this prayer suggests, beauty even in the unbeautiful?

The morning prayer is written by Monica, a producer at the American Museum of Natural History, where she creates educational materials for kids, families, and teachers. Originally from Hong Kong, she has been in New York for more than 30 years. She became a Christian in 1997, during the summer that she first attended Redeemer.

"I don't remember the first time that I prayed. But looking back, God has put many Christians in my life. During my first summer in New York City, a friend from elementary school invited me to a Christian summer camp—it could've been then! All I remember is that I came home from camp with lots of 'Jesus loves me' stationery and bug bites."

The heavens declare the glory of God; the skies proclaim the work of his hands.
Day after day they pour forth speech; night after night they reveal knowledge.
They have no speech, they use no words; no sound is heard from them.
Yet their voice goes out into all the earth, their words to the ends of the world.

PSALM 19:1–4

LORD, THE UNIVERSE is yours, and everything in it—our world and all who live in it. For you put the stars in their places, and they shine and dance for your glory. Your voice commands the morning, and the birds chirp, the trees sway, and the clouds swirl in an endless song to you.

God, who am I compared to your majesty? I am dirtier than the darkest soot, chained and broken. And yet, Father, you call me your beloved child. You redeemed me and made me beautiful and clean, as white as snow. You remind me that you make beautiful things. You make beautiful things out of the dust.

Father, you gave us eyes to see and hearts to perceive. Would you forgive us for not recognizing you in this world that you have made? You have given us minds to discover and the tools and ingenuity to study the universe and everything within it, and yet we are often so blind and hard-hearted toward the possibility of you in your workmanship.

God, would you give us curious minds and open hearts to observe and interpret your world? Would you fill us with your Spirit, so that as we discover you in your artistry, we may join in the eternal song of your creation?

Thank you, Father, for making beautiful things. Thank you, Jesus, that out of love for us you became unbeautiful, so that we became beautiful forever. And thank you, Spirit, for transforming our lives into a beautiful, joyful song for you. Would you help us worship you by showing your loving-kindness, generosity, and hospitality to everyone in our city: those who are our neighbors, those who will settle here, those who are just touring through. I pray that whatever they are seeking from this city—whether it might be artistic inspiration, distraction, or truth—may they find what truly matters: you.

Father, thank you for calling us to be a part of your plan for beautifying your city, so that it, along with the heavens, will declare your glory and proclaim the work of your hands, day after day, night after night.

In Jesus' name we pray, Amen.

TWENTY-SECOND DAY
EVENING

Simul justus et peccator. Simultaneously just and a sinner. This phrase is one of the great summaries of our faith. It means that we are both sinful and yet justified by Jesus' work *at the same time.* How is this possible? Because God is both just and merciful at the same time. He is just—he does not let sin go unpunished—but he is also kind, and he took the punishment on himself. As we think about the role of law in society today, how might we envision a culture that similarly upholds both justice and mercy? The attitude of this writer may be a start.

The evening prayer is written by Christian, an attorney practicing commercial and white-collar litigation at a large law firm in the city. He began worshiping at Redeemer in 2005 and now serves as an elder and as a Community Group leader. He and his wife, Jennifer, have three daughters and live on the Upper West Side.

"I think of my father every time I pray the Lord's Prayer. One of my earliest memories is praying it with him at age five or six."

God presented Christ as a sacrifice of atonement, through the shedding of his blood—to be received by faith. He did this to demonstrate his righteousness... so as to be just and the one who justifies those who have faith in Jesus.

SELECTIONS FROM ROMANS 3:25–26

OUR FATHER, God of justice, holy and merciful, gracious in all things, I thank you that I have a security and identity that cannot be lost, even if I lose my clients, my job, my license, or my life. Work in me as you see fit.

I thank you for providing order amidst the chaos of our sin. Though human laws and institutions are broken, through your grace they provide a measure of stability and justice in a fallen world. Today I pray:

For all lawyers, and especially those who follow you, that they would have diligence, creativity, and perseverance, and that they would seek justice above all things. Properly order their roles as zealous advocates, officers of the court, colleagues and friends, and as sinners saved by grace. When they lose, let them not be bitter. When they win, let them not puff themselves up. Let them never belittle their adversaries. Help them appreciate and honor their support staff. Help them to communicate clearly, set appropriate boundaries, and take ethical positions becoming of your children.

For judges, prosecutors, police, juries, defense counsel, prison staff, and probation officers: Give them wisdom and humility, that they would seek justice and love mercy, and not build a name for themselves at the expense of criminal defendants. Thank you for their service. Keep them safe.

For victims and their families: Let them find restoration and justice through a broken system, but also find their way to forgiveness and grace.

For criminal suspects, defendants, and prisoners: Give them confidence that they bear your image, and knowledge that when their dignity is violated, you are offended.

For the guilty: Bring justice, personal conviction, repentance, humility, and knowledge that they are forgiven through Christ's substitution.

Jesus, you were innocent but made yourself guilty for our sake. You perfectly upheld the law, even the law's requirement for punishment. Yet you perfectly and mercifully took the punishment yourself. May we, too, increasingly find opportunities to reflect your mercy and justice in our lives.

In the name of Christ, our Advocate before thy mercy seat, Amen.

TWENTY-THIRD DAY
MORNING

This writer begins his prayer acknowledging God's creation of the stars and ends it with a call for racial reconciliation. Somewhere between the celestial bodies and our bodies, things have broken down. And though we may constantly be at work repairing the damage, there is a lot to work through. Our problems are large, but never too large for the One who made the very air we breathe.

〜

The morning prayer is written by Jeff, a native of Ghana, West Africa, who lived in Los Angeles most of his life before transferring with his company in late 2011 to New York City. Here, he met his wife, Elena, and the couple had their daughter, Sofia. Jeff has been a member of Redeemer since early 2012, serving on the Diaconate and the East Side prayer team. Jeff worked as a financial and risk-management auditor, but in 2015 began to attend seminary: "After short-term trips to various African countries, I noticed a need to invest in the sustainable growth of African pastors and Christian leaders as they serve God's kingdom. I am pursuing a Master's of Divinity and my wife a Master's in Marriage and Family Therapy.

"When I was young, I read that Jesus instructed people to go to their closets and pray in secret. Zealous, I literally went into my bedroom closet before school, shut it behind me, and prayed. These were the most memorable first times of feeling like I was truly praying."

The heavens declare the glory of God;
the skies proclaim the work of his hands.

PSALM 19:1

O HEAVENLY FATHER, the heavens are the work of your fingers, as are the moon and the stars, which you have set in place. The earth is yours and the fullness thereof, the world and those who dwell in it. You summon the earth from the rising of the sun to its setting.

Thank you that in this vast universe, you remain mindful of me and provide for all my needs. Thank you that you have provided me with teachers, friendships, and a place to worship. You are so good to me. Please teach me how I can carry the burdens of others in prayer. On my block and around this neighborhood, please make me a caring and attentive neighbor.

Father, every good and perfect gift comes from you. Your Son laid down his life for us that we may lay our lives down for others. As I give myself to the needs of our church and our city, thank you that you are faithful to replenish my cup and provide for my own needs. Help me now to think of ways I might practically serve my neighbors today.

Silence.

Thank you that Christ, though he was rich, for our sake became poor so that by his poverty we might become rich.[2] Likewise, may you help me to thoughtfully consider the needs of the poor and the sick around me, to not ignore them, but to serve and love them in practical ways.

Father, righteousness and justice are the foundation of your throne. I pray that your kingdom will be reflected in our nation as we consider the confusion and pain regarding racial violence and discrimination. Thank you that in your loving-kindness you institute the authorities that we are under. Help us to pray and honor them. I pray that our justice system will be equitable for all people groups. Where there are injustices, let us lead the advocacy for change. Thank you for saying you will never leave us nor forsake us. Amen.

James 1:17, 2 Corinthians 2:8–9, Psalm 89:4

TWENTY-THIRD DAY
EVENING

We tend to be black-and-white in how we think about people. *That one is a poet. That one is an analyst.* Yet such distinctions are often misleading. What about the one who is both a poet and an analyst, like the woman who wrote this poem? The truth is, God made all of us both with minds that think and hearts that feel. We all have both left and right—logical and intuitive—sides to our brains. And Jesus has called us to love the Lord with *all* our hearts and minds, not just a part of them.

❧

This prayer was written by Rebecca, a health services researcher. She moved to New York City from Boston in January 2015.

"I grew up in the church, though I first sought God's will for my life in my early twenties. I can't really say I remember my first prayer."

Joshua went up to him and asked, "Are you for us or for our enemies?"

*"Neither," he replied, "but as commander of the
army of the LORD I have now come."*

JOSHUA 5:13–14

WHO AM I TO ASK
   if you are on my side?
Lord, am I on your side?
Help me be so confident in you
   that I can give love without
      needing anything in return
Let your presence become so near
   that distance from others is
      something I don't fear
Reveal your character to me,
   so that when feelings come and go,
      I will always be rooted in you

Each day that passes,
   there's another closed door
   sometimes I wonder if You will
      allow much more
Yet my failed will
   only makes me more sure
   You are breaking my heart
      to make it pure
And maybe there was no other way
   to get me to this place
   than to shake my reality
      so I'd turn to your face

Because before the pain
   I didn't understand
   that everything I am
      is in the power of your hand

This battle for my soul
   has gone on for so long
Stripped bare
   Becomes clear
      it's only you to whom I belong
And now when my actions are set apart
   from what I want to do
   it's your Spirit in me, reflecting you...
So after all these tears
   and broken years
   after all the memories, all the fears
Deep in my heart
   lies this simple prayer:
   At the end of the day,
      I want to hear you say:
      "I loved you all along"

TWENTY-FOURTH DAY
MORNING

Brokenness has multiple meanings. To be broken is to not work properly. Coffee makers and television sets can be broken. Brokenness can also mean a lack of wholeness. Bones and windows can be broken in this way. Theologically speaking, we may speak of the world as broken by sin in that it does not work quite how it should. Injustice and suffering are effects of the fall and will one day be erased. We may also call ourselves broken in that we lack wholeness and integrity, our lives shattered not just by the fallen world outside of us but by the selfish pride and ambition within us. This writer offers a prayer for restoration and for healing.

The morning prayer is written by Julia, who is from Dallas, Texas, and moved to New York City in June of 2010. She is a liver doctor, splitting her time between seeing patients, doing research, and teaching in an academic setting.

"The Center for Faith & Work (CFW) is the arm of Redeemer that appealed to me most initially; service to the church through CFW programming naturally followed suit. After completing the Gotham Fellowship, I began praying for my industry (health care) and institution to remember its original calling.

While I don't recall the content of my first prayer as a four-year-old, I do recall the quality: there was a sense of fervency and deep yearning that serves as a spiritual memory even now."

In repentance and rest is your
salvation, in quietness and trust is your
strength, but you would have none of it.

ISAIAH 30:15

O H FATHER, we are so broken. Some of us have broken genes, others body parts, others whole organ systems, and others broken lives and broken hearts. Some days, we all have broken spirits. I pray for us all, and today I specifically lift up _____.

When you allow me the privilege to enter into the brokenness of someone's life, remind me that it is indeed a privilege. Protect me from being overwhelmed by the brokenness in them and help me to remember the brokenness in me. Keep me humble and close to you, if not in body, then in spirit. Lift my head periodically. Inspire me with hope through your Holy Spirit so that I can communicate that hope to the ones in front of me—the ones you have called me to learn from, collaborate with, teach or heal.

Forgive me for too often trying to tackle things on my own. Help me yield the day, these lists, these tasks—these overwhelming tasks—to you. Open my eyes, Father, unstop my ears, and unfetter my heart by showing me the ways you seek to unburden us from the heaviness of our load. Death is heavy, Father.

When my day and hands get busy, please remind me of your grace that has allowed me to develop and cultivate skills for your glory. Help me to have a quiet and trusting mind and heart despite tragic and confusing situations. You have called me to so much, Father, and equipped me well, yet I often focus on my own shortcomings in meeting the needs that surround me. Please help me to realize that my decrease and your increase is worth seeking and finding. Your burden is light.

God, give us your grace this day. Give it through the hands of doctors and nurses and housekeepers and volunteers; give it to the minds of researchers and scientists; give it to the spirit of the brokenhearted throughout this place and this city. May we all hear your life-giving words even in life-ending circumstances. Teach us how to love one another as you have loved us. O Great Healer, heal us. Amen.

Matthew 11: 28–30

TWENTY-FOURTH DAY
EVENING

Our culture prizes the bright and brilliant, the clever and the strong. So we spend much of our lives avoiding failure, humiliation, and disappointment. When they come, we want to crawl under a rock and hide. Yet sometimes it is in these times that we feel the love and grace of God most poignantly. We have a God who does not judge us by our performance but by the performance of his Son. This writer reminds us that even when we fall, underneath us are the everlasting arms of God.

The evening prayer is written by Lois, a counselor, licensed marriage and family therapist, and clinical director who has been working at Redeemer Counseling Services for more than 17 years. She regularly teaches classes on gospel transformation at Redeemer and has been involved in equipping pastors and leaders to do pastoral counseling in Germany, Holland, Argentina, Cuba, Mexico, and the Dominican Republic. She especially loves to travel yearly to the land of her birth, Cuba, to be a part of God's work there.

"I was five years old at the People's Church in Toronto, Canada, during a children's meeting. I invited Christ into my life."

Since then we have a great high priest who has passed through the heavens,
Jesus, the Son of God, let us hold fast our confession. For we do not have a high priest
who is unable to sympathize with our weaknesses, but one who in every respect has
been tempted as we are, yet without sin. Let us then with confidence draw near to
the throne of grace, that we may receive mercy and find grace to help in time of need.

Hebrews 4:14-16

JESUS, THANK YOU THAT YOU ARE my great high priest, who, having passed through humiliation on earth for my sin, has been exalted to the right hand of God where you are interceding for me.

I have tasted humiliation. There have been times when my heart has frozen; I have wanted to run and hide, to unsay my words. I have experienced the looks, the silence. The disapproval left me feeling so unloved, shameful, and misunderstood. If only people could see how hard I am trying to do the right thing! But no matter what I do, it's never good enough, cool enough, or smart enough.

So I draw near to you. To whom else shall I turn? You know. You've been there. You get me. You care. You sympathize with my weakness. You live to make intercession for me—a human in heaven, nail-scarred hands, Son of God, having been tempted just like me, yet without sin. Thank you that you invite me to come near your throne in these moments of fear and shame, and you welcome me, without reproach, with your mercy and grace.

Thank you for helping me see that where I fear to go, you have already been. You were "despised and rejected by men; a man of sorrows, acquainted with grief; as one from whom men hide their faces, you were despised, and we esteemed you not." As I experience my wounds, I am getting a small taste of what you went through physically, emotionally, socially, psychologically, and spiritually on my behalf. You were wounded for my transgressions, crushed for my iniquities.

You're the reason to visit my old wounds, for in doing so, we will cry together, fellowship together as fellow sufferers, and I will be able to know you deeper, comprehending through my suffering a little of your suffering on my behalf. You use my sufferings to thrust me into your very own heart of love. What wondrous love is this, O my soul! Amen.

Isaiah 53:3

TWENTY-FIFTH DAY
MORNING

This is a creator's prayer, written as a request that God would bless one's creative effort. Creativity comes not just in the writing of plays, the composition of melodies, or the application of paint to canvas. Creativity is the process of bringing something new into the world, whether it is a new way of thinking, a new analysis, a new business, or a new work of art.

The author of this prayer preferred to remain anonymous in hopes that the reader would focus more on the prayer than the author.

He who was seated on the throne said,
"I am making everything new!"

REVELATION 21:5

MY FATHER AND CREATOR, Make a tabernacle of my heart. Hoist the joists to shed light into each chamber's dark corners, that your radiance might shine through me, from you, and onto this divine empty space.

Beat in me that divine rhythm (that only you can so generously impart) where creativity occurs outside the linear curse of time, where work finds the groove that stops all seconds from ticking, where I lose myself and find your spirit.

May the blood, breath, light, and word of Christ flow through me—the same that put a song on David's lips, that brought life to dry bones before Ezekiel, that make forests sing, that make bushes blaze, that lead me beside still waters. May I create from this and nothing less.

And when I hit the inevitable wall, remind me that the best work begins and ends from awe. Leverage my frustration, sin, and anguish, and make a furnace from my struggle, wherein dross falls and saviors dance and the elegance of a core that holds all together is revealed.

Abolish from me the haunting urge to direct praise toward myself, to solve divine mysteries with crude reductions, to face limitations with envy instead of creativity. When I practice structure, let me see the cross. When I employ craft, let me remember your handiwork. When I yearn for greatness, let your vastness be my imagination's raceway.

As I create, may I follow your lead and make the process personal—sacrificial in its risk, daring in its scope—and find empathy from incarnation (what was it like, Creator, to step into your own creation?) and in so doing, honor your image inside me.

Hear this petition, oh God, that is so riddled with my sin. Purify it with your grace. Use the morsel of goodness that resides in my work as a speck of yeast that might beget transcendence, lift the veil of this world, and see what is unseen.

Thank you for being more faithful to me than I am to you. Thank you for every mystery, miracle, beauty, truth, and grace you've shown me that has inspired me to create. Thank you that my king, comfort, savior, friend, and father is also the Original Artist, by whom all is made, in whom all holds together, and to whom we lift up our hearts for your dwelling. Amen.

TWENTY-FIFTH DAY
EVENING

When Jesus taught the disciples to pray, he taught them to address God as "Our Heavenly Father." The name is intentionally personal. God offers himself to us as the Father of fathers. Just as all people here on earth are made in God's image, all earthly fathers in some way should reflect our Father in heaven. This prayer, originally written for Father's Day, asks for blessing for all those fathers.

❧

The evening prayer is written by Holly, who is from the Pacific Northwest. After a handful of stints abroad, she came to New York in September 2013 (after seven years of wanting to) and started attending Redeemer about a month later (after not planning to attend at all). She is an editor for a Latin American policy group.

"My first prayer was in the van with my mom, driving down Tracyton Boulevard, and asking Jesus to live in my heart. As a four-year-old, I imagined this meant I could look down anytime I wanted and wave at Jesus, who'd be sitting with his cup of coffee in the kitchen section of my Polly Pocket-shaped heart, reading the newspaper."

One day Jesus was praying in a certain place. When he finished,
one of his disciples said to him, "Lord, teach us to pray,
just as John taught his disciples." He said to them, "When you pray, say:
'Father, hallowed be your name, your kingdom come...'"

LUKE 11:1–2

LORD GOD, I praise you and I thank you that, of all the names we could use to address you, your Son Jesus taught us to call you "Father."

Father God, today, I offer a special prayer for the fathers in our church—both spiritual and familial. I pray for those who have been fathers, who are fathers, and who will be fathers. Thank you for the gift of fatherhood and the blessing it is to be raised and loved by an earthly father, and how it is a model for us to know and feel how you, our Heavenly Father, love us and continually seek our best.

Father God, I pray, when and where there's been hurt and sin and brokenness between fathers and children, that you by your Holy Spirit would, in your kindness, bring us to repentance and reconciliation and, if you'd have it, restoration.

Father God, I pray for the women in the church, that you would give them your heart to encourage the men as they walk out, in humility, strength, and grace, to the calling you've placed on their lives as sons, brothers, husbands, and fathers.

Father God, I pray for the single mothers in this city. I pray that you would be their strength and peace as they work to fill two roles, as they raise their children in the absence of their children's fathers. I ask that, if it's your desire, that you would give them husbands, men who love you and who desire to love and serve these women and their children, and to share in the joy and labor of raising their children with them.

Father God, I pray for the children in our city today who do not have a father in their lives. I pray that you by your Holy Spirit would minister to them in ways that are too deep for words. I pray that you would give them a vision and a hope of who you are as a Father to them, that they would know they are loved infinitely and intimately by you.

Father God, you've given us everything you have—even your own Son by his costly, precious death on the cross—all so that we could be adopted into your family and be called into a glorious, eternal inheritance with you. I praise you and I love you and I give you my life to be used so that you might be glorified in my life and in this city. Amen.

TWENTY-SIXTH DAY
MORNING

Much of the unhappiness in our lives and the short-sightedness of our thinking might be ascribed to our failure to wonder. The very fact of existence is an extravagant and shocking idea. If we properly stood in wonder about our place in the world, we might be less self-centered and more willing to spend ourselves on behalf of others, as the author of this prayer aspires to do.

The morning prayer is written by Eva, who lived in Taiwan, Utah, western New York, Boston, and China before graduate school studies led her to New York City in 2011. Eva was first introduced to Redeemer by listening to Tim Keller's sermons overseas and became involved at Redeemer upon moving to the city. She now serves as the director of Redeemer's W83 Ministry Center.

"My first prayer was when I was eight years old. I recall being at a Pioneer Girls' meeting (like Girl Scouts, but with Bible verses. No cookies; just merit badges). I prayed with one of our group leaders to accept Christ."

But as for me, my prayer is to you, O LORD.
At an acceptable time, O God, in the abundance of your
steadfast love answer me in your saving faithfulness.

PSALM 69:13

MERCIFUL FATHER, THANK YOU for the gift of life and for mercies that are new each morning. Thank you for the daily miracles: those that I acknowledge and those that I don't. I confess that my heart often grows hard, O Lord—sometimes sour, sometimes disappointed, but more often than not, just plain tired.

Fill me, O God, with wonder. In the sun's reflection through a pane of glass, the birds chirping with the first signs of spring, a child walking hand-in-hand with his parent—fill me with wonder. In the bricks, the sidewalk cracks, the subway trains, and rushing crowds—fill me with wonder. Even in the downcast head, the cardboard signs, the sad eyes—fill me with wonder. And fill me with compassion.

Give me neither fluff nor naïveté, O Lord, but a true wonder that spreads across my heart and chest and causes me to pause and take notice.

Fill me with a sense of who you are—the weight of your name and the fullness of your presence.

Fill my darkness with your light. Fill my loneliness with your hope. Fill those moments when everything feels like nothing or when the world is so beautiful that my heart aches and my body yearns for more.

Fill the places that seem so empty. Fill the spaces where words fail.

Fill me so that, as my cup overflows, I may pour out onto others and pour these blessings back at your feet. May the wonder you reveal take me outside myself. In my work and personal life, may the sense of your wonder manifest itself through the practices of hospitality and active care; may I be one who welcomes and includes strangers instead of demanding that others include me.

May I follow in the path of Jesus, who welcomed the sinners and the tax collectors. In you, Jesus, may I find my ultimate fullness, for it is only in you that I move and live and have my being.

Amen.

TWENTY-SIXTH DAY
EVENING

Throughout the Bible, those who are spiritually lost are often called "blind," while those who are spiritually found are described as regaining their sight. Paul's conversion came with the scales falling from his eyes. Just as we ought to thank God for the gift of physical sight, we ought to ask God for the gift of spiritual sight—seeing things, ourselves included, as they really are in light of who God is. Spiritually speaking, we are often unaware of our own blindness. We must, as this prayer does, ask for our eyes to see the paths God has prepared for us.

The evening prayer is written by Sarah who writes about sight from professional experience as an optometrist on the Upper West Side. She was born and raised in a small town in western New York state, "surrounded by farmland and cows."

"I moved somewhat unwillingly to the big and scary city of New York for optometry school, and now I've been here for nearly seven years. I began attending Redeemer soon after moving to New York, and the relationships I've made there through the Community Groups (including meeting my wonderful husband) have been a huge source of encouragement to me and a major reason why I've decided to stay long- term in this great city.

I grew up surrounded by Christian family, so prayer was definitely part of my childhood from a very young age, but the first time I remember praying on my own as a way of talking to God was probably not until I was about 12."

The Lord is my shepherd, I lack nothing. He makes me lie down in green pastures, He leads me beside quiet waters, He refreshes my soul. He guides me along the right paths for his name's sake. Even though I walk through the darkest valley, I will fear no evil, For you are with me.

PSALM 23:1-4A

ALL-POWERFUL AND HOLY GOD, how is it that you love me so deeply? Though I am not deserving, you are always near me; you protect me, you guide me. You promise to care for me and lead me as a good shepherd watches over his sheep—you provide for me all that I need. I praise you for the times in my life I can look back and see you were at work and for the plans I know you have for my future.

Even though I know of your promises to protect and provide for me, I struggle with giving you control and surrendering to your leadership. I fight for independence. I think I know what is best for my own life, and I make decisions based on my own understanding and desires without consulting you. I am like a sheep heedlessly running away from the care of his shepherd—forgive me, Lord, for my wanderings.

Forgive me for looking for satisfaction from earning success at work and praise from others, as these things fail and leave me feeling unvalued and alone.

Instead, remind me constantly of your loving presence so I can be freed from feelings of worthlessness and worry. You know how I struggle with speaking out for you when I know I should, and I ignore your nudges to do what is right when the rest of the world says doing what's wrong is OK. Forgive me, and when the next time comes for me to choose between following you or following the world, fill me with courage fueled by your faithfulness.

God, I ask that you would continue to guide me and protect me. Remind me over and over again of your promises to provide for me and watch over me. When I feel as though I'm stumbling blindly through life, open my eyes to see your direction and the paths you've prepared for me. When the darkness of this broken world brings me to despair, share with me your vision of your kingdom and fill my soul with the true peace, rest, and life-giving joy that can only come from you.

In Jesus' name I pray, Amen.

TWENTY-SEVENTH DAY
MORNING

James tells us that true religion is helping orphans and widows in their distress. Is that statement to be taken literally, or are orphans and widows stand-ins for all people in distress? For centuries, the church has cared for the disadvantaged. But we must ask ourselves: Are we doing our part? Are we waiting for the marginalized, orphans, and widows to knock on our doors for assistance? Should we seek them out? Perhaps we could at least begin by regularly praying for them by name, as this writer does.

～

The morning prayer is written by Deborah, an artist and art therapist who has worked with Redeemer's children's ministry and Community Group ministry. Born and raised in New York City, she moved away for college and lived in other cities before returning to the city in 2013, when she became a member at Redeemer.

"I became a Christian when I was 11 years young. I first truly prayed when I was four years old and could not sleep because I was terrified to be alone in the dark. I was in my room, and my dad prayed with me through the fears and into peace."

Lord, you have been our dwelling place throughout all generations.
Before the mountains were born or you brought forth
the whole world, from everlasting to everlasting you are God.

PSALM 90:1–2

OH, EVERLASTING GOD,
You call us to return to you
Our secret sins are revealed
in the light of your presence
Forgive us and teach us your wisdom
Satisfy us with your steadfast love
so that we may rejoice and be glad.

Your Word says that perfect love drives out fear, but there are some who would use fear to drive away love. Lord, I pray that you bring an end to the violence, killings, and fear being perpetrated by those who would be terrorists.

I pray that you remove corrupt leaders and raise up to leadership men and women of integrity and love for their people. I pray that our national leaders would make decisions for the long-term good. I specifically pray for

_____.

I pray for the weak, the vulnerable, and the powerless, the poor, the foreigner, the infirm, widows, and orphans. In this city I specifically pray for _____. I pray for your protection over them; we pray for your consolation, restoration, and safety.

God, let your work be shown to us. Lord, let your glorious power be seen. I pray that you bring spiritual revival to our city. I pray that our city becomes a city known for the good care of its citizens as much as it is known for its wealth, glamour, and entertainment. I pray that you transform us into good neighbors.

Let your favor rest upon me and establish the work of my hands so that I remember that I depend on you. I pray that I might do my part to create thriving friendships and a community among the people in your church. I pray that those who suffer would not be alone. I pray that you would bring many people to know your love and worship you. I pray that we would be overflowing with hope everyday by the power of your Holy Spirit.

In Jesus' name I pray,

Amen

TWENTY-SEVENTH DAY
EVENING

Two percent of all students in America attend New York City public schools. They are our future—but they are also our most vulnerable citizens, as this writer, a teacher, knows well. As she prays for our children and their teachers, she recognizes God as the greatest teacher—the perfect role model for all of us.

The evening prayer is written by Karis, who was born in Rochester, New York, and raised in a Christian household. She moved to New York City in 2013 and has been teaching in high-need public schools in Brooklyn. She co-leads a Community Group in Jersey City with her husband.

"When I was five, I remember praying to receive Jesus three times because I was so anxious that he wouldn't accept me: several times at various children's camps and once alone in my bedroom. Now I know that I didn't need to be anxious. He did it all for me, once and for all."

Yet to all who did receive him, to those who believed in his name,
he gave the right to become children of God.

JOHN 1:12

DEAR FATHER IN HEAVEN, Thank you that you are a God who loves and understands children. You see them as a blessing, not a burden. Indeed, you promise your kingdom to them, and you rebuke those who try to keep them from you. Be not far from the young students in this city. Many of them struggle for deliverance from poverty and homelessness and shame. Thank you that you judge all people with equity, and that you deliver the oppressed. Do not let our children flounder in our flawed educational system. Rather, grant them your strength to crush the enemies of justice.

I pray that you would especially watch over our students' choices and keep them from harm: When they are tempted with gossip, grant them forgiveness; when they are angered to disobedience, grant them wisdom; when they are incensed with rage, grant them peace; when they are weighed down by apathy, grant them courage and strength. Do not let anyone cause these little ones to stumble—instead, put them on a path where their talents can be harnessed to their fullest potential. Let them be image bearers of you and your glory. God, I specifically pray for _____.

I pray for all our teachers. Thank you for those who serve sacrificially, giving of themselves for their students. Forgive them when they fail to treat the students as you would and use them to teach our children well. I pray that you would grant these teachers your self-sacrificial forgiveness, and I ask for it myself. Show us by example what your mercy looks like.

Let me meditate on your word day and night and take refuge in you, not myself. Help me to look to your example as the greatest teacher: You grew frustrated, but not harsh. You were disappointed, but never cruel. You taught by example and through stories, not by force.

Grant me joy in serving you! You are the strength of my heart. Sustain me, sustain the teachers, and sustain all students in this city as we struggle toward your kingdom coming.

Amen.

No person is so far from God that she or he is irretrievable. Indeed, Jesus seemed to take particular delight in those whom others might have considered lost causes—prostitutes, the sickly, those who couldn't make their marriages work. As this prayer emphasizes, we are all prodigals who have wandered from the true way and need a savior who will come after us and not let us go.

The morning prayer is written by Ellie, who grew up in a small dairy farm town in Connecticut. She came to New York City in the late 60s and landed a lead role in "Jacques Brel is Alive and Well and Living in Paris." In 1977, she cofounded The Actors Institute and later created an intensive for cabaret performance at the Eugene O'Neill Theater Center.

"Failed marriages led me to look for solace in all the wrong places. But when a boyfriend brought me to Redeemer in 1992, I heard Tim Keller and was drawn by the questions and the warmth of the people to re-evaluate the secular views I had and became a believer in 1994. I do not think I had ever prayed to Jesus before I came to Redeemer. I think I realized that I could pray 'Lord, help me' and it would be sufficient to be called a prayer."

"Sir, give me this water so that I won't get thirsty and have to keep coming here to draw water." He told her, "Go, call your husband and come back." "I have no husband," she replied. Jesus said to her, "You are right when you say you have no husband. The fact is, you have had five husbands, and the man you now have is not your husband. What you have said is quite true."

JOHN 4:15–18

L ORD, I PRAISE YOU for rescuing prodigals like the Samaritan woman and me from lives of never-ending self-indulgence.

The woman at the well strayed far from the path of holiness with her many affairs. When I think about her, I marvel at your respect, your love, and the listening ear you gave her even though you already knew about her considerable shame. May I be as kind when I meet others who have taken the prodigal road, who have strayed far from the path of holiness. May I remember your kindness when I see that prodigal is me, for I too have strayed.

God, I pray for women everywhere who are faced with unwanted pregnancies, accidental pregnancies, pregnancies they are tempted to end. They may have no one to talk to. They may find it impossible to see beyond their shame and humiliation. But you know their anguish. Let them know your gentleness. Open their eyes to the hope you carry for them. Protect them.

You have protected me in this city, even though I have used it to run after indulgence. You never let go of me until I met and acknowledged you and was able to admit and confess my shame and experience forgiveness. I am thankful and amazed that you placed me in a loving and gracious circle of friends. Use me and my redeemed life story as a testimony of the amazing power of your deliverance and love. Let me be honest about my past, so that I can give you more honor for your deliverance.

Jesus, I pray that by your model of personal intimacy, respectful interchange, tender teaching, and loving rebuke of the woman at the well, you would also use my life to bring hurting people to faith and offer your loving-kindness to those you send to me.

Lord, I praise you for pursuing me, for protecting me, for providing for me, and making yourself known to me just as you revealed yourself to the woman at the well.

Amen.

TWENTY-EIGHTH DAY
EVENING

C.S. Lewis called pride the great sin, the "complete anti-God state of mind." It is the sin underneath so many other sins—the idea that we do not need God, and that the world revolves around us. If it feels like a less embarrassing sin than others, it is only because we don't have a good enough grasp of how heinous it is to God. This prayer asks for God's mercy to fight this fundamental and dangerous mindset.

❧

The evening prayer is written by Gregory, an otolaryngologist (ear, nose, and throat doctor) and head and neck surgeon. He was born in Harlem, grew up in central New Jersey, and returned to New York in 1996 to start his ENT residency. He first attended Redeemer in 1997 when he was brought by a medical student.

"I became a Christian here and was baptized in 1999 at age 29 by Tuck Bartholomew. My first true prayer was in 1999, after one of Tim Keller's sermons in Hunter College auditorium. During the sermon, he challenged the congregants that, based on what Jesus said, you had to either believe or not believe that he was the Son of God. I prayed for the ability to believe."

He must become greater;
I must become less.

JOHN 3:30

HEAVENLY FATHER, Thank you. For being here. With me. Right now.

Each time I intend to pray, I find it difficult to start. You are all-powerful and all-knowing, so you must already see my worries, my heart, and my struggles. I struggle especially with one of the "deadly sins:" pride. I think more highly of myself than I ought. When I think of Jesus' example, I am humbled. Why do I not think of it until it is too late? This pride is poisonous. You know how it affects how I see myself and how I interact with others.

Yet even as I say these words, I feel that it is not enough that I just confess my sins. I have confessed them before, but it seems like I revisit these sins daily, despite my best efforts to correct them. I feel like a record that keeps skipping to play the same tune, over and over again.

Lord, I earnestly ask for your help in overcoming these sins and ask that you help change my heart, so I will not be prone to repeating them. Help me find a better way, a way more in line with your son, Jesus. Help me become saturated in your Word so that my thoughts and actions are more like his and not like the evil within me.

Almighty Father, you know that during the busy workweek, I am prone to forget your presence in my life. I ascribe my competence to my abilities and knowledge and give you short shrift. Please send me the Holy Spirit to remind me that any abilities come from you—that they are God-given.

And please especially help me to see you, not just during this time of prayer, but in the nooks and crannies of the days to come.

I pray this in Jesus' name.

Amen.

TWENTY-NINTH DAY
MORNING

For New Yorkers, few things are scarier than the idea of failure. This is a city filled with people determined to make it. To fail in any area of life, personal or professional, threatens our identity. But as the psalmist says, all our good lies in the Lord. As this writer contemplates, because of the cross, we need not fear failure, but can place our identities fully in Christ.

The morning prayer is written by Eugenia, a poet who says she has had an on-again, off-again relationship with Jesus since the age of 13. Her first book chronicles part of that tumultuous journey. A 2014 Gotham Fellow through Redeemer's Center for Faith & Work, Eugenia lives and writes in New York City, where she now understands that despite her skepticism, God never viewed their relationship as "off-again."

"I remember praying facedown in bed as a child in an abusive home. The first time I 'truly' prayed was at age 12 in a bathroom, where I read: 'I asked Jesus, "How much do you love me?" "This much," he answered. Then he stretched out his arms and died.'"

*"I say to the Lord,
'You are my Lord; apart from you
I have no good thing.'"*

DEAR GOD,
Some days the word I use to describe myself is "failure." I start to believe I am failing at everything. I'm thinking not only about my work, but also about my family. About the ways I squander my time, my money, my heart. The ways I fall short of everyone's expectations of me in my work and as a friend, a sibling, a daughter, a partner, and decent human being.

What did you see in me that made me worthy of your life? I need to hear you tell it to me again—that most excruciating yet comforting truth: that you died for me simply because you created me and you love me. Father, tell me that you "demonstrate [your] love for us in this: while we were still sinners, [you] died for us."

The apostle Peter, after all his bold confessions of allegiance to you, betrayed you as you predicted he would. And yet as Peter came to terms with his failure, you performed your greatest act of love on the cross for him and for all those who would continue to let you down. Let me see how that same grace extends to me.

Teach me, Father God, that my worth has nothing to do with anyone's expectations—or even my own expectations—of me. Cement into me the truth that even when I fail to meet *your* expectations that I love you and love others, you still delight in me, not because of anything I've done, but because of what you've done to make me acceptable for your kingdom. Today, I ask instead that you deepen my understanding of my worth in your eyes. Help me, Father God, to recognize and take pride in my one true identity as your beloved, your child.

Peter failed you, and yet on him you said you would build your church. God, I pray that you would use failures like me to help build your church now. We will fail you, but you can work even through our failures. Build your church. Plant many more in this city. For your glory and in Jesus' name I pray, Amen.

Romans 5:8

TWENTY-NINTH DAY
EVENING

In one of the earliest accounts of his teaching, Jesus went to the synagogue in Nazareth and read the scripture from Isaiah: "The Spirit of the Lord is on me, because he has anointed me to proclaim good news to the poor. He has sent me to proclaim freedom for the prisoners and recovery of sight for the blind, to set the oppressed free, to proclaim the year of the Lord's favor." After he read, Jesus declared the scripture fulfilled in hearing it. He was the one anointed to proclaim the good news. This writer calls for the generous justice of Jesus to move in our time.

The evening prayer is written by Vanessa, who was born in New York City, grew up in upstate New York, and lived for more than a decade in the Boston area before returning to New York in 2011. She grew up attending a Chinese church, where she became a Christian as a teenager, after returning from a youth conference. Vanessa has been attending Redeemer regularly since the spring of 2013.

"I first truly prayed while traveling in Romania as a 20-year-old college student on a mission trip. Because I was alone in a country where English wasn't the primary language, I began to write conversations to God in my journal out of loneliness. I still journal prayers to this day."

"I say to God my Rock, 'Why have you forgotten me?
Why must I go about mourning, oppressed by the enemy?'"

PSALM 42:9

LORD, I COME TO YOU always with concerns about how my life will turn out. My desire to feel loved, my desire to feel fulfilled at work. I become sorrowful and downcast. Yet I know that compared with many in the world, even my brothers and sisters in faith, my troubles are light. When I hear about your children around the world who are suffering terrible ordeals, even subjected to horrifying abuse through sex trafficking, I am reminded that parts of the world are darker than my darkest days. I ask for mercy for them, and for justice.

I have known what it means to have interviews not turn into jobs. To be passed over. Many tonight are unemployed or underworked. May they find a calling and the joy of work that brings self-respect. There are some who are in jobs they would rather not have, jobs filled with conflict and disappointment, jobs that demand more life than they give. God, lift our heads to discern your call to be faithful even in the difficult hours and give us courage to know when to change.

I have known loneliness and know that many others tonight are lonely. They have prayed for someone to love and partner with in marriage. They wonder if they will always be alone. They are tempted to feel forgotten by you. God, have mercy on their anxious minds.

God, I can be tempted to feel worthless and forgotten by you. Like Hannah, who was barren and mocked for years, her prayers unanswered. Yet I remember the words of the psalmist:

Why, my soul, are you downcast?
Why so disturbed within me?

Put your hope in God, for I will yet
praise him, my Savior and my God.

May I yet praise you. My life is more than marriage or work or these other things I chase after. My life is in you. You are the rock, the firm foundation on which my identity is grounded. Help us to trust you, even during our journeys through the desert. Refine me and prepare me for what is ahead.

Thank you, Lord, for always being with me and loving me with an everlasting love. Resource me with your love, so that, through it, I can love you and others. Amen.

Psalm 42:5

THIRTIETH DAY
MORNING

This writer touches on our culture's fascination with beauty and asks God to help us pay attention to what our hearts are drawn to so that disordered loves don't tear us apart. Beauty and fashion can celebrate the God who represents all goodness, beauty, and truth. But fashion can also be used to hide the real us, to cover our shame. The author here prays for a right approach to beauty.

✺

The morning prayer is written by Chantal, who became a Christian at age 10 in Arizona where she spent most of her childhood. During university, she studied abroad in South Korea, where she met and married her husband, Andrew. She now resides in New York and works as a trend forecaster in the fashion industry. She is grateful that not only New York, but also Redeemer, has felt like home for the past eight years.

"I was raised by Christian parents so prayer was always a natural part of my life. I was in fourth grade when I began to understand that God was listening and would answer my prayers. I am still awed by what an intimate form of communication prayer is!"

"You are the portion of my inheritance and my cup; you maintain my lot. The lines have fallen to me in pleasant places; yes, I have a good inheritance."

PSALM 16:5–6

O GOD, YOU ARE an amazing God. You are at once personal and mighty. Your awesomeness invokes fear, but you say I can approach you as your child. I cry out, *"Abba*! Father!"

Despite my neglecting time with you in favor of spending my time on more worldly pleasures, the Holy Spirit reveals your wisdom to me through your Word. It is living, and I am humbled by your revelation to me on such a personal level.

Thank you for your patience and constancy. In a material world where I often forget that you are Lord over all, I am tempted to "hasten after another god," but you always redirect my path.

God, thank you that I am fulfilled when I rest in the fact that "you are the portion of my inheritance and my cup; you maintain my lot. The lines have fallen to me in pleasant places; yes, I have a good inheritance."

Our culture is obsessed with beauty. We spend so much time and money making ourselves presentable, attractive. We create beautiful clothes but know that even the best dressed among us are only approaching the elegance of the lily of the field, which you clothe in effortless beauty. Meanwhile, this over-emphasis on beauty has left countless people struggling with pornography, eating disorders, or the shame of feeling unlovely. We desperately need to hear what you've told us—that we are beautiful in your sight. Lord, help us!

It is mind-boggling to me that you can be so gentle, merciful, and loving but also sovereign, just, and righteous. Even during my darkest hours, you are abundant in grace and mercy. You guide me through painful moments; you gently show me that you are sovereign. You are my Lord. You allow me to question you, to doubt you, and you still love me. Your love for me while I was yet a sinner—it is hardly comprehensible.

It is through this love, and in the name of Christ Jesus, I pray. Amen.

Psalm 16:4

THIRTIETH DAY
EVENING

This prayer demonstrates how prayer need not be compartmentalized to narrow categories of interest. In these few words, the writer prays for everything from the Middle East to the creative work of artists to the local church.

The evening prayer is written by Julia, who is from Kansas and moved to New York City in the fall of 2012 for an acting conservatory. She began attending Redeemer immediately after moving here, began serving children's ministry in the nursery shortly thereafter, and then joined the staff in 2013. When not at Redeemer, she spends most of her time babysitting and auditioning.

"God calls artists and has made it abundantly clear to me that my art is really his. The first time I truly prayed, I was 16 years old and was away at boarding school. It was a difficult season in my life, and I really learned that Jesus was the only One who was going to bring me comfort and peace."

Do your best to present yourself to God as one
approved, a worker who does not need to be ashamed
and who correctly handles the word of truth.

2 TIMOTHY 2:15

GOD ALMIGHTY, I praise you for your grace that covers my sin and washes away my shame. Forgive me for my selfishness, my self-sufficiency, and my pride. Thank you for the cross, Jesus. Thank you for taking God's wrath so that we might be with you forever. Oh Lord, open my heart more and more to the ramifications of what you've done for us. You died for all people, Jesus, so open my heart to lovingly pray for all people:

I pray for all the oppressed. Comfort the refugees, those who have faced violence, those who are persecuted for their faith in you. Please bring your glory and peace to the Middle East. I pray that you would miraculously change the hearts of those who preach terror, that they might see that you are truly the way, the truth, and the life. Show those who would do violence everywhere that you love them. You died for them just as much as you died for me. Forgive me when we mercilessly demonize them, because I fear them, or because I feel I cannot show them love.

Father, I pray that your truth go forth. I pray that you would be the center of our workdays, that we would glorify you in our work. As we move through our city, we know you are here. We know that this place is not "godless." You are on every street, every avenue, and every subway.

I pray especially for your Spirit to move among artists and be present in their art. Artists are creators. We are made in your image. May artists everywhere create *for* you and *because* of you. May we remember that no critic defines our worth. You alone do. May I remember that too.

Jesus, I pray for your Church. I pray for all those who love you and are meeting in secret because it is unsafe to do so openly. I pray for our church and for the other churches in this city. I pray for our church leaders. God, please inspire them. May they know and teach your word with thanksgiving. May we be your hands and feet in this world. May we spread your good news. Show us new ways to serve you and your children. Take us to the homeless and the needy, to the widows and the orphans. Grow us in prayer, love, sacrifice, and praise. Thank you for all these things and more, Jesus. In your holy name, Amen.

THIRTY-FIRST DAY
MORNING

Christians know that Jesus died for their sins and saved them from ultimate judgment. However, many Christians still live as if they are being judged and look to their work as a form of justifying themselves. The secret is to learn how to work as an act of service and gratitude to God rather than as an argument justifying one's own existence. This writer asks for assistance in doing exactly that.

❧

The morning prayer is written by Amilee, the assistant director of the Center for Faith & Work at Redeemer, focusing on training and equipping New Yorkers in integrating theology and practice. She facilitates learning, organizes lay-led vocational intensives, and supports Redeemer's Gotham Fellowship leadership development program. Amilee, her husband, Dan, and their strong, spunky daughter, Olyvia, live on the Upper West Side.

"I can't remember my first prayer exactly. But I was at my parents' home recently and found a prayer journal from when I was probably about eight years old. I do remember my father helping me write an entry each night—a praise of thanksgiving for prayers answered, and a new request."

Teach us to number our days,
that we may gain a heart of wisdom.

PSALM 90:12

F ATHER—
Daily I rise, and even if my head acknowledges your faithfulness and unfailing love in providing a new day, my heart quickly takes control over the minutes and hours ahead. The wrestling match begins: Time vs. Me. I am attempting to do more than I possibly can—a limited being attempting to fulfill an unlimited number of responsibilities. I find myself falling behind at every turn.

I have lived for so long under the weight of this idol of Pride, operating as if success is self-made, hard work gets it done, and that with enough effort, I can tackle any challenge and solve any problem I encounter. Break down my pride. Forgive my presumptuous sins, and show me that I am not capable but for your grace, your strength, and your power at work in and through me.

I long for the sweet breath of your Spirit, empowering, renewing, and enlivening me. Allow me to rest within the limitations you've placed on my life, seeing them not as limiting, but as uniquely designed for limitless

flourishing. You yourself took on the limitations of human form, knowing exactly what kind of transforming work could be accomplished in a concrete number of days, hours, minutes—the length of time that Christ himself walked this earth. Who am I to cry out, "I need more time today! My work's not done!"?

May I recognize how desperate I am for your grace at work—grace giving me eyes to see the brokenness needing to be addressed in my workplace, and grace endowing me with the ability to enter in and serve the work, according to your divine purposes.

May the same grace that appeared in the person of Christ to redeem this world— the work of your hands!—be the grace that operates in and through me as I go about the work of my hands. Grace that knows no limits, yet chooses to operate within them, carrying forth your work of renewal in this city, even as we long for the new city that is to come.

In Jesus' name, Amen.

THIRTY-FIRST DAY
EVENING

If we are made in the image of God, we are made in the image of a creator. We are all creators. In that sense, then, the questions posed by this writer are relevant for every one of us: "My Maker, what am I to make? My Creator, what am I to create?" Few of us think of ourselves as artists, but we are all creators who make use of the time and talents we have. The question is what will we make of our time? May what we make of it be beautiful, true, and good.

~

The evening prayer is written by Melanie, a singer-songwriter and worship leader who works in communications and fundraising for Redeemer City to City. She is originally from Falls Church, Virginia.

"I came to Redeemer the first time the Sunday after 9/11 because of the tragedy of the attacks. I had an experience with Jesus Christ while sitting in Hunter College in October of 2001. I don't remember the first prayer I prayed. But as an adult, I found a childhood journal in which I asked God to be real to me. I don't remember ever writing that or wanting that, so it was very dear to me to find."

"And he who had received the five talents came forward, bringing five talents more, saying, 'Master, you delivered to me five talents; here I have made five talents more.' His master said to him, 'Well done, good and faithful servant. You have been faithful over a little; I will set you over much. Enter into the joy of your master.'"

MATTHEW 25:20–21

DEAR LORD, to you be all the glory, honor, and praise.

My Maker, what am I to make? My Creator, what am I to create?

You built me for a purpose and you gave me ability. You gave me talents. You designed me so that I breathe, my heart beats, my eyes open without thought. Because you designed me this way, I am free to make and to create. So it is with all of us. You have given gifts to every person.

But what am I to make? What am I to create? What is my calling now?

Today, my Maker, may I join you to create something of eternal significance? You are God, and you can make something from nothing. But I can't make anything from nothing. I need you. I need help, inspiration, strength, courage, materials from the earth. I need whispers from the angels. I need your Holy Spirit to collaborate with me.

Would you free me from fear? When ideas come, would you give me the reason and plans to support them? When discouragement comes, would you protect me? When my hands don't work, would you unclench them, cure them, and strengthen my hands to be like new? When the Accuser tells me I will amount to nothing, that my efforts are all in vain, and that everything I do is dumb—would you say to me: *Well done?*

Today, my Maker, I commit to you my doings, my creations. With your help, I make and give to others. I make and give back to you. Amen.

CONTRIBUTORS

ABOUT *the* EDITOR

Maxwell Anderson began attending Redeemer in 2002. He has served as an elder, an advisor, and as a community group leader. He lives on the Upper West Side with his wife Jessica and three children, Carolina, Gracie, and Sam. Maxwell is the author of *The MBA Oath: A Higher Standard for Business Leaders* (Penguin Portfolio 2010). His blog and newsletter, *The Weekend Reader*, covers technology, culture and the meaningful life. He is CEO of Stagecoach Ventures.

ABOUT RISE

The Rise Campaign is the first phase of a decade-long project to grow the body of Christ in New York City in order to help the city prosper. Our belief is that if there were far more Christians and churches in the city who loved their neighbors, cared for the poor, shared the good news, and integrated their faith into their work, then not only would our neighborhoods be improved, but the entire culture of the city also would be lifted.

ABOUT REDEEMER

Redeemer Presbyterian Church was planted by Tim and Kathy Keller in 1989. The church exists to help build a great city for all people through a movement of the gospel that brings about personal conversion, community formation, social justice, and cultural renewal. Redeemer will soon become three churches—East, West, and Downtown—and then intends to multiply those three churches in the coming years into several more. No one church, no matter how big, is big enough for New York. A city this rich in cultures and neighborhoods needs hundreds of churches to serve all the people.